"This book 'Hidden Thorns' is an encouraging and remarkable story of how a courageous mother coped with the murder of her daughter.

The story describes in detail all the sad travails that life has unfairly dealt the Author. Especially sharing how she handled the tragic senseless murder of her beautiful daughter. No one ever fully recovers from the agony of the death of a child. But this mother wanted to be someone who was happy and not hiding from the world, bitter and angry. Forgiveness was the way to peace—and she knew she would need that, but how could she forgive her daughter's murderer?

Over time, she came to realize that there actually was a small miracle happening; her daughter was taken from a place of violence, where she was all alone, to a peaceful place in eternity. What this individual did was horribly wrong, but did she want to be defined by her worst nightmare? How is that any kind of compensation to a mother for the loss of her daughter? And did she want that to be the way she lived for the rest of her life?

What the Author has shown us is that the most important thing anyone can do in life is what God has given us to do here, now or whenever. She has demonstrated clearly that she has been more courageous than anyone I know in letting God write her story. So, my congratulations go to her for being a faithful obedient servant, as painful as it was.

This book of diversity in the face of tragedy makes for compelling reading."

– *D.C. Harris-Hughes, B.Ad. Voc.Ed - RN*

"I was profoundly moved by the author's courage and honesty. Her story will support and help to heal others. I regard it as an honour that she entrusted me with her heart in these pages."

– *Professor Newell W Johnson, CMG, FMedSci*

HIDDEN THORNS

HOW DO YOU FORGIVE YOUR DAUGHTER'S MURDERER?

HIDDEN THORNS

A TRUE STORY

MARIE-ROSE FOX

Copyright © 2018 Marie-Rose Fox

ISBN: 978-0-6485913-0-6
Published by Challenger II Pty Ltd
Warwick Queensland 4370
Australia
www.marie-rosefox.com.au

 A catalogue record for this book is available from the National Library of Australia

All rights reserved. No part of this publication may be reproduced, stored in a retrieval system or transmitted in any form or by any means, electronic, mechanical, photocopying, recording or otherwise, without the prior written permission of the copyright holder. The information, views, opinions and visuals expressed in this publication are solely those of the author(s) and do not necessarily reflect those of the publisher. The publisher disclaims any liabilities or responsibilities whatsoever for any damages, libel or liabilities arising directly or indirectly from the contents of this publication.

I dedicate this book to my daughter Michelle,
my beautiful Christmas angel.

Thank you for giving my life purpose and
in turn making me a better person.

Without you my world is like a day without sunshine.
I miss you and your infectious smile.

I will always love you my darling.
You are forever in my heart.

RIP

Contents

Introduction xi
1. The Alarming Call 1
2. The Puzzle which Followed 7
3. State of Origin 13
4. Searching for Michelle 18
5. Mystery, but for One 25
6. Turning Back Time 30
7. Overcoming the Odds! 36
8. Unveiling the Past 42
9. Facing Reality 46
10. New Beginnings 50
11. A Different World 57
12. The Unbreakable Bond 62
13. A Call to Obedience 67
14. Adam's Confession 73
15. The Senseless Feud 79
16. A Double Whammy 84

17.	Inevitable Guilt	88
18.	The Last Straw!	91
19.	Wounded to the Core	97
20.	An Unbearable Task	102
21.	Ineffable Times	107
22.	Goodbye, my Angel	111
23.	My New Normal	115
24.	Extending Forgiveness	120
25.	A 'Country' Change	125
26.	Love and Peace	132
27.	New Storms Ahead	137
28.	Duty of Care	142
	Epilogue	148

Introduction

I've always loved the name my parents chose for me - Maria Rosa - in the original Portuguese of my birthplace, but quickly abbreviated by my parents and family to Rosinha, which translates to "little rose". Once we left Portugal for France, then later Australia, I became Marie-Rose, the name I am most comfortable with after six decades. But to my extended family, I am still Rosinha—little Rose.

I love the name Rose because of the images it evokes. Sweet fragrances. Beautiful colours. Soft and silky to the touch.

But looks can deceive, and though a rose is so beautiful, it also has sharp thorns that can be very painful if you're not careful. You might not even notice the thorns until they pierce your skin and make you bleed.

Like the flower for which I was named, my own life has been filled with many beautiful aspects. A tightknit family. Adventure and travel to a magnificent new continent that became my home. A precious daughter. A loving husband. Work I enjoy and excel at. A lovely home. When people come to know me and view my life, they may even see only the beautiful, fragrant aspects of it.

But also like my namesake, my life has been filled with hidden thorns, some of them so painful it is still hard to talk about them.

HIDDEN THORNS

Thorns of betrayal and rebellion and broken relationships. Thorns of my own sin. Thorns of words said or not said, of things done or not done, that I regret to this day.

And the most painful thorn of all that still stabs my heart with agonizing pain, no matter how many years have gone by. In brief, my world changed dramatically ten years ago when I lost my only child to murder. In a moment, I not only lost my beautiful daughter but any hope of becoming a grandmother to her future children.

Still, I didn't go through this horrifying ordeal alone. I was blessed to have *at* and *on* my side the Creator of roses with all their beauty and thorns and the Creator of this *rosinha*, known more commonly as Marie-Rose Fox. The presence of God, my loving heavenly Father, is the only reason I was able to come through this experience to where I am today—sane, healed, and whole.

When terrible tragedy enters our lives, those around us often don't and can't understand what we're experiencing because they haven't been through it themselves. This leaves us feeling very alone, frightened, and lost. When I felt like this, not knowing what to do or who to turn to in order to go on living, God's Holy Spirit stepped in to help me deal with the situation. I remain in absolute awe at the significant transformation for which God is responsible in my life.

The presence of a loving heavenly Father doesn't mean God will take away all the thorns from our lives—or that he took away mine. In the New Testament, the apostle Paul himself, one of God's greatest servants, shares vulnerably and intimately in a letter he wrote to the Corinthian church of a "hidden thorn" in his own life that he begged God repeatedly to take away (2 Corinthians 12:7-10). Instead of granting Paul's request, God gently reminded him, "My grace is sufficient for you, for my power is made perfect in weakness" (v. 9). The apostle went on to say:

Therefore I will boast all the more gladly about my weaknesses, so that Christ's power may rest on me. That is why, for Christ's sake, I

Introduction

delight in weaknesses, in insults, in hardships, in persecutions, in difficulties. For when I am weak, then I am strong. (vv. 9-10)

Like the apostle Paul, I still bear hidden thorns that have left me scarred and wounded. But also like the apostle Paul, in my weakness and pain and grief God has always been there to give me strength and comfort. In fact, that is the reason I am now taking up pen and paper—or rather a computer keyboard—to write my story. The Bible tells us in that very same letter the apostle Paul wrote to the Corinthians that God gives us comfort in trials, not just for our own benefit, but so we may then turn around and comfort others:

Praise be to the God and Father of our Lord Jesus Christ, the Father of compassion and the God of all comfort, who comforts us in all our troubles, so that we can comfort those in any trouble with the comfort we ourselves receive from God. (2 Corinthians 1:3-4)

So I tell my story today, not for any personal benefit, attention, or glory, nor even just to get it off my chest. I tell it first of all so other mothers and fathers and family members who have experienced traumatic loss may receive the comfort I have received. So they too may learn the truth I have learned that life can and will go on even when horrible tragedy strikes for what appears no real reason.

I am also writing for every reader in need of God's comfort and strength, whether they've gone through tragic loss or some other difficult life experience. Maybe you are someone who has been used or abused. Or whom society has forgotten. Maybe people around you are too busy to care for your needs. Yes, this could be you!

My ultimate hope and prayer in relating my story to you is that it will help you, my reader, deal better with your own life's challenges. Your own hidden thorns. I am inviting you to tap into what I call my source of sanity, even survival, when things become unbearable and I think I can't go on anymore. That's when God can and will intervene.

So let me encourage you to continue reading my story because I cared enough about you to write it. That said, please don't think for a minute that writing this book has come easily! No, this has been by far the hardest thing I've ever done in my life. But God has made clear to me that the time has come to open my heart and share intimately and vulnerably with you, my reader, my entire story just as I experienced it, hidden thorns and all. Nothing more. Nothing less.

Because this isn't about me. It isn't even about the loss of my only child. It is about how a loving heavenly Father was there for me in the depths of my loss, grief, and depression, and how he can help you too in your time of trauma and pain and need—if you will just let him.

Ravi Zacharias, well-known Christian speaker, author, and theologian, expresses this perfectly in his sermon "The Meaning of Life" (YouTube, August 11, 2017):

> "You know you always think you're going to manage your life in your own way. It never works. The most important thing in your life is to find that intimacy with God, and he will guide you, he will hold you, he will take you through safely in your journey hand in hand with him. When everything comes together, then you have wonder. Then you have truth. Then you have love, and you have security. That's what gives life meaning! And you'll find that only God is big enough to do that for you."

On that note, let us not wait a minute longer in getting on with my story.

1

The Alarming Call

It was the middle-of-the-night call every parent dreads.

"Good morning. This is the Helensvale police calling." The voice on the line was male and authoritative. "Am I speaking with Michelle Rigg's mum?"

Helensvale is a suburb of the Gold Coast, a coastal region and popular surfing destination in the Australian state of Queensland not far south of Brisbane, Queensland's capital. It was also where my twenty-eight-year-old daughter Michelle lived with her long-term boyfriend Adam, just a half-hour drive from our own neighbourhood.

But why would their police station be calling me at 2:30 a.m., much less asking about Michelle? An anxious knot was already tightening my stomach as I answered, "Yes, this is Michelle's mum. Is there anything wrong? Why are you calling me at this hour in the morning?"

"Sorry about the early hour, ma'am, but I have to ask you a couple of questions. Have you spoken with or seen your daughter recently?"

In reality, it had been a long time since I'd either spoken to or seen my daughter, perhaps the longest in either of our lives. There were reasons for the estrangement, but these were hardly the business of some stranger even if he was a police officer. So I responded with my own query. "No, why?"

Ignoring my question, the police officer went on, "When was the last time you heard from her?"

By now I was getting seriously worried. The duplex my daughter had recently purchased was in a newer suburban development, safe and quiet most of the year. But this was early Tuesday morning, November 27, 2007, a significant date for two reasons. First, at this time of year and all the way through the Christmas holiday season, the Gold Coast exploded with activity as a huge influx of teenagers poured in for the annual Schoolies celebrations.

For non-Australian readers, this is a week-long holiday for students who have just completed their Higher School Certificate (Year 12) exams. Tens of thousands of graduates from all over Australia travel to Surfer's Paradise, the heart of the Gold Coast, or other Gold Coast hot spots for a week or two of fun and relaxation before heading off to a job or university or whatever the future holds.

Ostensibly, they are there to enjoy the beach and surf (the year-end holiday season south of the equator being the height of summer as well as end of the school year), along with theme parks, shopping malls, and other attractions. At this time of year, the glitter of the holidays can be seen everywhere. Department stores, small shops, restaurants, and public places are all adorned with lights and Christmas decorations. Christmas carols can be heard on every street corner, and the Christmas spirit is well and truly ablaze.

But as might be expected when thousands of young people are celebrating their freedom, Schoolies celebrations also have a reputation for a lot of alcohol, illegal drugs, and wild parties, much like spring break in North America or Europe. Which in turn generated an annual uptick in crime, drunken accidents, and other social problems.

This year, the Schoolies excitement had been compounded by the upheaval of Australia's federal elections, which had taken place on Saturday, November 24th. It had been an exciting week since the Labor Candidate, Kevin Rudd, was a Queenslander born and bred.

1 | The Alarming Call

There was great rejoicing Saturday evening throughout Queensland when we learned that the Labor Party had won by a landslide and Kevin Rudd was our new Prime Minister.

But that too meant lots of celebrations, which placed even more impaired drivers on the roads. Had my daughter encountered such a situation? Or even been partying too freely herself?

"Why?" I asked again. "What's happened? Has Michelle been in an accident?"

This time the police officer took time to answer me. "We don't know, ma'am. She was reported missing last evening. At this stage we're just contacting her family and friends. Can you tell me just when it was you last saw her? Or spoke to her?"

Now I was truly alarmed. A stranger or not, this was clearly not the time to withhold our personal family drama from the police.

"Well, I actually tried calling her just this evening," I explained. "Her birthday is coming up soon in December, and I was hoping to set a date to celebrate her birthday together as a family. But all I got was her voice mail."

Just remembering that call brought a lump to my throat. Whatever the personal drama that had alienated my daughter and me, Michelle was my precious "Christmas gift" from God, who had been the joy of my heart from the moment of her birth. The Christmas season was her own favourite season of year, and no matter what was going on between us, celebrating her birthday together had always been a special bonding time for us. Our current estrangement had gone on too long, and I had already decided that planning a special birthday dinner with her, whether at my own home or the restaurant of her choice, would be the opportunity to restore our broken communication.

When Michelle hadn't responded to my call, I wasn't particularly worried since the entire month before Christmas in Australia is typically filled with office parties and other holiday fun. A very popular girl, my daughter was constantly receiving invites from friends and colleagues, so I simply assumed she was out at some social event. I'd planned to try calling again in the morning. She would surely be home by then to feed and walk her beloved Staffordshire Bull Terriers, or "staffies", as she called them, Tyson and Ninja. I knew she would never neglect them for any party.

"The last time I actually spoke to Michelle was a few months ago," I went on to admit. "As to when I last saw her in person, that was some six months past at my brother's funeral in Sydney. I am sad to say we had a serious fight then and haven't been on speaking terms since. I do know she was planning to travel to Sydney sometime in December for a Christmas and birthday celebration with my mum—her grandmother—and other family members who live there."

I knew this because my mum was in regular communication with both of us and always kept me up to date on my daughter's activities. Mum might not always agree one hundred percent with how I handled my relationship with Michelle, but she always backed me up, and I appreciated that. The mention of travel plans brought to mind a new possibility—my ex-husband Jack and Michelle's adoptive father, with whom my daughter often maintained a closer relationship than with me.

My anxiety eased fractionally as I shared my thought with the police officer, "You know, it just occurred to me that maybe Michelle decided to fly down early to surprise her father. He lives in Sydney too, and today is his birthday. You might want to try contacting him."

"Ok, we'll do that."

"Would you like his number? I have it in my contacts. I'll get it for you."

"No need for that, ma'am. We have it right here on Michelle's mobile."

With that statement, my anxiety again shot through the roof. "What do you mean, you have it on her mobile? Hasn't she taken it with her? That's odd! Michelle doesn't go anywhere without her

1 | The Alarming Call

phone. It's permanently glued to her ear. Something must be wrong!"

"Well, her partner Adam has just been explaining to us that the two of them had a row Friday night, and she stormed out of the house without her phone."

It was only now that I realized the police officer must be calling from Michelle's own home. He went on to give me further details. According to my daughter's boyfriend, thirty-six-year-old Adam Cartledge, Michelle hadn't taken her car when she stormed out but had told him she was going for a walk. Adam had figured she needed time alone to cool off, so he hadn't followed her or been overly-worried about her wellbeing. When she never came home that night, he'd assumed she was still too angry to want to see Adam, so she'd decided instead to go visit a friend or her mum—me!

Adam himself had left to spend the rest of the weekend with friends. It wasn't until he returned home Sunday night that he'd discovered Michelle still wasn't home. On Monday morning around 10 a.m., he'd received a call from Michelle's boss, asking why she hadn't shown up at work. Only then did it occur to Adam that something might be wrong, so he'd called the police to report her missing.

I found out later that Adam hadn't actually reported Michelle missing of his own accord. When her boss had called her home to find out why she hadn't shown up for work, Adam had given him the same story he'd later told the police. Immediately skeptical, her boss had told Adam plainly that he needed to call the police. If he didn't, her boss would. Other friends had also become worried over the weekend and had been calling around, concerned over her disappearance.

Only under her boss's threat and the recognition that there was already an uproar over Michelle's absence had Adam called to report her missing. Even then he had waited until 9 p.m. Monday evening. The reason he gave to the police was that he'd still been hoping she had just gone somewhere in a temper and would return on her own once she cooled down.

It had been after midnight by the time the police arrived at the home Michelle and Adam shared. Their concerns had been immediately raised when they found my daughter's mobile phone sitting on the counter. They also found her car parked in its normal position and her two dogs Tyson and Ninja corralled out in the yard. This had also raised concern since even if she'd gone off with a friend, it seemed odd she would have left her dogs there unattended with Adam also gone for the weekend.

I was just as skeptical of Adam's account. I was also now very angry and worried. "My daughter wouldn't go off for a walk on her own to begin with without taking Tyson and Ninja along with her," I told the police officer flatly. "She's too smart to be walking alone without protection this time of year. And are you telling me Adam waited the entire weekend before he called to report her missing?"

"It isn't uncommon for partners to take off after a row," the police officer told me reassuringly. "Even for a weekend or longer. That your daughter never showed up for work nor notified her boss that she would be absent is a bigger matter of concern. But maybe she's with a friend or in Sydney, as you said. I'll give her father a call right now. In the meantime, please don't worry too much. I'm sure she'll turn up soon. In my experience with this same scenario, I've often seen people turn up after three or four days safe and sound."

"I hope so. Please call me as soon as you find her. In the meantime, I'll make a few calls myself. Good night. Sorry, I mean good morning!"

I hung up the phone, wondering if I was awake or having a bad dream. This was like something you'd see in a crime drama like *Law & Order*. It couldn't possibly be real!

2

The Puzzle which Followed

I headed back to my bedroom. I knew I hadn't been dreaming when my husband Stephen asked me who had called. I explained that the Helensvale police were asking all sorts of questions about Michelle and that she'd been reported missing. Stephen was optimistic.

"Look, darling, it's late. I'm sure it's a misunderstanding," he said encouragingly. "She was probably having too much fun at some Christmas party and decided to crash at a friend's place till the morning. Don't worry! I'm sure she'll turn up soon enough."

I wasn't so easily comforted. "Yes, that's what I initially thought too. But the constable said she'd had a fight with Adam on Friday and stormed out of the house on foot. And now they've found her phone inside the house. She would never go out without her phone. Nor would she walk alone at night without taking her dogs along for protection. Not in a million years! I'm telling you, something doesn't add up!"

"So why don't you give Adam a call and get his side of the story?" Stephen suggested. "If the police were over there before they called you, he's likely still awake."

That made sense, so I did. The phone rang only twice before I heard the familiar deep voice of Michelle's boyfriend. "Hello?"

"Hi, Adam, it's Michelle's mum here. Sorry to phone you at this early hour of the morning, but I just received a call from the Helensvale police asking me a whole lot of questions about Michelle and stating that you reported her missing."

"Yeah, the police just left the house," Adam admitted. "They were here for a while asking questions."

"So what happened?" I demanded. "Why did you wait so long to report her missing?"

"Well, like I told the police, we had a huge fight on Friday night, and she left," Adam admitted. In my mind's eyes, I could picture him clearly standing in Michelle's kitchen, phone in hand, a tall, well-built man who had always loomed over my petite, slim daughter. Eight years older than Michelle, Adam had never been as successful in his career or finances. But he'd always seemed a quiet, placid person, and to all appearances had absolutely adored my daughter. Michelle had always seemed equally happy with him.

"I didn't go after her because I thought she needed time to clear her head," he went on. "When she didn't come home, I figured she didn't want to face me, so she'd gone off to see you or another friend. But when she didn't turn up to go to work on Monday, I started getting worried and called the police."

"She went out on a walk without taking Tyson and Ninja?" I broke in heatedly. "That doesn't make any sense, and you know it! And why would she not take her mobile? Now tell me what really happened! For one, what were you fighting about? What made her leave the house on her own? And when exactly did she leave? I want to know! You've had disagreements before, and she never went missing for three whole days. Besides, if she wanted to clear her head, why didn't she just get into her car and go for a drive?"

"How would I know?" Adam's normally calm tones were now angry and contemptuous. "As to why we quarreled, she was getting herself all dolled up to go out with that rich boyfriend of hers. Or

2 | The Puzzle which Followed

didn't she tell you we broke up more than two months ago? Oh, yes, I'm still here sleeping in the guest bedroom only because she needs me to pay half the mortgage. Not to mention looking after her dogs while she goes to Sydney next month, since she's insisting if I can't come up with the rent that I do odd jobs to work it off, like I'm some kind of personal handyman! Anyway, she got all dressed up, did her hair, even painted her finger nails and toenails, the lot! Why shouldn't I be angry? She never did that for me!

I could hear from his quick, heavy breathing on the phone, his clipped speech, just how angry he was as he went on, "Besides, she was constantly taking me for granted, asking me to do work around the house and all that. I wasn't happy, but when I told her I was fed up, she told me to mind my own business. We weren't an item anymore, so she could do whatever she pleased in her own house.

"That's when I lost it, and we had a big fight. Okay, so maybe I smashed a couple of photo frames on the floor. And, yes, when she kept on yelling at me, I pushed her away. She might have tripped and hit her head just a bit. But she got right back up again, so she was clearly just fine. She really did need to cool down. You know how she is! So when she said she was going on a walk to get some fresh air, I gave her space. I guess she was just too worked up to think about taking the dogs."

"And you just let her go like that?" I interrupted him again, livid. "All upset and hurt in the dark without her mobile? Are you crazy? You know the kind of activities going on out there with the elections and Christmas holidays. And let's not forget the Schoolies! Anything can happen to an attractive young woman walking alone at night this time of year. Especially with the highway so close to the house. She could have been kidnapped, raped, who knows! Didn't you think about any of this, Adam? If you didn't have the guts or decency to go after her yourself, why didn't you at least call me?"

"Well, you two weren't on the best of terms. Besides, I figured she would turn up soon enough when she was ready to come home."

"So you waited three whole days to report her missing? What is wrong with you? I can't believe this! Do you want to know what I think? I think you're an absolute moron! Your priority should have been her safety. Never mind that we weren't communicating. She's my daughter, and you know that Stephen and I would have gone looking for her, no matter what, if only you'd called."

"Don't worry. Michelle is a big girl." Adam's tone didn't sound in the least bit concerned. "She wouldn't do anything silly. She'll turn up, you'll see!"

"Let's hope so, Adam, for your sake," I responded furiously. "In the meantime, what are you doing about it? Are you helping the police with their inquiries?"

"Well, I already told them everything I know. They said not to leave town while they're investigating. And they took her mobile in case someone calls. Mine too. They'll get back to me when they find Michelle." His voice softened fractionally. "I really do hope she's okay. I know I should have gone after her, but I was really mad at her for getting all tarted up for that rich guy. Anyway, I'll get her to call you when she comes home."

If this was his version of an apology, I was not buying it. Something just wasn't adding up. I *knew* Michelle wasn't in a good place. I could feel it in my bones.

"Adam, I can feel your anger. I hear it in your voice too!" I said warningly. "And I still can't believe you waited this long to report her missing. Is there something you're not telling me? Go on, say something. There's more to it than you're ready to admit to, isn't there?"

When he made no response, I slammed down the phone in his ear. "Aaaarrrgh!!!!!"

I was furiously angry now as well as worried, and there was no way I could go back to sleep. Returning to our bedroom, where Stephen was still awake waiting for me, I sat on the edge of the bed and quickly

2 | The Puzzle which Followed

shared my phone call conversation with Adam. By the time I finished, I was so agitated that Stephen urged me, "Try to calm down a little. There's nothing you can do right now, so why don't you take half a sleeping tablet. It would do you good. I've just taken one."

Taking the tablet, I hopped into bed. We talked for a while longer as Stephen was still trying to calm me down. But his tablet was taking effect, and within fifteen minutes he'd fallen asleep. Conversely, sleeping tablets have never worked for me. Still unable to sleep, I looked at the clock and wondered if I should call my sister Gloria, who was Michelle's godmother and lived in Sydney. If Michelle really had gone to Sydney, Gloria might know where she was.

Despite the late hour, my sister answered the phone almost immediately. I explained why I was disturbing her at this time of night. First the phone call from the police. Then my conversation with Adam. Gloria understood my concerns completely. Then I asked if she'd heard anything from Michelle there in Sydney. Not that I really had any hope after my conversation with Adam that she'd simply flown down for her father's birthday and forgotten to let her boss know.

"Actually, yes," she responded. "I got a call from her last Friday just before she left work. She was looking forward to a Christmas party she would be attending that night with an old friend named J*. She also mentioned that the party was being held on a yacht."

That cleared up one mystery. "So J* is the rich guy Adam was referring to! I know him. He's a nice guy. He and Michelle are old friends who've known each other for years. There's nothing romantic between the pair, just friendship. Why would Adam be so jealous over that?"

"Why don't you call J* and talk to him?" Gloria suggested. "He would know if she ever showed up at the party."

"I don't have his number," I declined. "Besides, the police are calling all her contacts right now. I hope there's a good explanation for all this, but I don't like it."

"Don't worry so much," Gloria encouraged me. "She'll turn up. Call me in the morning and let me know what happens."

"Okay, I will. But if she does call you, please let me know straight away," I said anxiously.

"Of course, that goes without saying."

After hanging up, I sat staring at the wall in our lounge room, where I had made the call, and tried to think rationally. I kept telling myself there had to be an explanation to this nightmare. There was no way my little girl wasn't coming home. She was too smart for that. She knew how to take care of herself. She would eventually turn up at home unharmed. She had to for me!

On the other hand, I couldn't dismiss the feeling that there was something very fishy with Adam's story. It just didn't add up. Even if he was telling the truth about the fight and that Michelle was fine when she left the house, there was no way she would have left without taking her mobile, if not the dogs. And her birthday was still weeks away. Despite my earlier optimism, it wasn't likely she'd have taken off to Sydney this early in the holiday season, especially without telling her boss.

I tried Michelle's phone again, though I knew the police had taken it into custody. But maybe she'd been found by now and they'd returned it. I'd hear her voice on the other end, and this nightmare would be over.

Instead, all I heard was her familiar voice message recording, one of those annoying silly ones with the voice of some cartoon character. If only she had recorded her own message, I would at least have had the comfort of listening to my precious daughter's voice. How had things come to such a pass with the person whose very existence had been responsible for the greatest joy and the greatest heartache of my entire life.

How had I let things come to such a pass?

3
State of Origin

To understand just how and why the birth of my precious "Christmas gift" was the most significant, and certainly the happiest, event of my life necessitates going back to my own birth and childhood. A childhood that at first glance might seem as idyllic as the one I had tried to provide for my own daughter. But as would be the case with Michelle, all was not as it seemed.

I was born in January 1953 in Famalicao, a small town near Porto, North Portugal. I was the youngest of seven children, so it is perhaps not surprising that my name was very quickly reduced to an affectionate diminutive—Little Rose, or Rosinha.

My older siblings were divided evenly—three girls and three boys. Our birth order went like this: Lily, Armando, Lourdes, Gloria, Tony, John, and yours truly. There is only a ten-year gap between my oldest sibling Lily and me, so we are all under two years apart, a challenge for my parents to keep fed and clothed. But large families were not uncommon at that time as there was no contraception available to country folk, and even if there was, my Mum, a devout Catholic, didn't believe in it. She welcomed each of her children into the world with a glad heart.

We lived on a farm my father had inherited when his own father passed away. So we never went hungry since the farm crops and an abundance of fruit trees provided ample food. New clothing, toys, or other possessions might be in scant supply. But for us children at least, farm life was idyllic as it provided abundant open space in which to play.

Since we didn't own a television, we relied on each other for entertainment. I was particularly close to my two youngest brothers, Tony and John, just three years and one year older than me. Like the Three Musketeers, we went everywhere together. John and I were the cheeky ones while Tony was more sensible, so we often teased him about taking things too seriously. He should relax and have fun, we told him. After all, you're only young once!

Since our parents couldn't afford toys, our solution was to make our own. Bows and arrows, slingshots, Billy carts, and even our own tree house were just a few of these. I hope you are taking a look through my rose-coloured lenses just to capture the essence of what a fun childhood we had.

Still, times were hard. To take ownership of the farm after my grandfather's death, my father had to buy out his siblings' shares of the estate. This necessitated borrowing a considerable sum, which had placed him in heavy debt while still only in his twenties. Even with the austerity in which we lived, profit from the farm crops and fruit harvest was not enough to pay off the debt. If my parents couldn't secure additional funds, the farm would have to be sold.

Dad was determined not to let this happen, so he decided to go to France and look for work. This was not uncommon, as good-paying jobs for countrymen were often more available in nearby countries than in Portuguese cities. My Mum's father had previously found good work in France, so that country was a logical choice for Dad.

It pained Dad to leave his family behind, but he saw no other option for keeping the farm, which was very dear to his heart. And he did

3 | State of Origin

return to see us whenever he could, usually at Christmas time. On one of these visits, he asked Mum to let my oldest brother Armando, then in his early teens, go back to France with him. This would allow my father to qualify for a housing commission unit in Oissel, a small town near Rouen, which is best known because Joan of Arc was martyred there, in Normandie, France.

Mum was reluctant, but agreed. Once Dad had saved enough money to buy train tickets, he made arrangements for the rest of the family to join him in France. It was 1959 when we left the farm to join my father in Oissel, and I was now six years old. We children were not happy about leaving the farm, since we loved it there. We weren't able to bring many belongings, which was perhaps just as well since we had nine people crammed into a three-bedroom apartment. With none of our extended family nearby, we felt far more isolated than on the farm.

Dad was the sole bread winner, and to support the whole family, he had to take a job in Paris, about a hundred kilometres from Rouen. This job paid well, but the distance meant he was once again separated from his family, boarding in Paris with a friend during the week and returning to Oissel only on weekends.

Even with better pay, my father's salary wasn't enough to provide well for nine people. The lack of money put great pressure on my mum, who struggled constantly to make ends meet. To help out, my oldest sister Lily as well as Armando, next in age and both old enough now to hold jobs, left school to contribute to the family's finances. As teenagers, they didn't earn much, but at least it helped somewhat.

During our first years in France, Tony, John, and I remained inseparable. With nine people living in one small apartment, there was no room to play inside. But behind the apartment complex was a large wooded area we liked to call our backyard. The only problem was that all the other kids who lived in the apartments played there too. My two brothers quickly took charge and formed two teams, the Cowboys and the Indians, based on John Wayne movies and other westerns they'd watched. John was Hawk-Eye the Indian Chief. Tony was John Wayne the Cowboy.

My brothers took their leadership positions seriously. This, of course, pitted one brother against the other, so I had to be the peacemaker. Most of the other kids were also boys, so I became very much a tomboy. You would never catch me wearing a skirt, and I never did own a doll or even play with one.

John was a natural "horse trader", as they say. He would make his own bows and arrows, then sell them to the members of his "Indian tribe" for extra cash. Tony made his own sling shots, but instead of selling them, he preferred to give them away to his team so they could defeat the "Indians" in battle. For bigger items like Billy carts and a treehouse, my two brothers would combine their expertise. The treehouse became their secret meeting place, and as their little sister I was the only girl allowed up there.

Being the trader he was, John never missed an opportunity to make money. Growing up in the country, he had an advantage over city boys, especially in capturing crickets, which were popular then among kids to keep as tiny pets. Albino crickets were the rarest, so they fetched double the price of ordinary brown ones. John would trap them in an empty match box of matches perforated with pinholes so the insects could breathe. He would then distribute them within his "tribe" to be sold around the community.

One day an interested young client turned up at our apartment, hoping to negotiate with the Chief himself. When Mum answered his knock on the door, the boy asked to speak to Hawk-Eye because he'd heard he could buy an albino cricket from him. Mum stared at the child, then turned around and shouted, "John, who is this Hawk-Eye, and what is this story about albino crickets?"

John quickly came up with an explanation that left Mum marveling at her youngest son's pure genius. Still, she wasn't going to let him get away with it.

3 | State of Origin

"Go to your room!" she ordered sharply. "And let this be the end of it, understood?"

It wasn't the end of his business. But from that day forward, all transactions were made at the treehouse so no one would get caught. I played only a small part in my brothers' business ventures, but they always included me, and it kept all three of us busy after school. Who needed store-bought toys when there was always something far more exciting happening day in and day out?

Two years after our arrival in France, Dad relented and bought the family a black-and-white television set, which really wasn't of much interest to us younger children. I have very fond memories of my years as a musketeer. We didn't have a lot, but it didn't take a lot to make us laugh, and we were very happy. At the end of the day, our childhood memories are the ones that will stay with you for the rest of your life and I wouldn't trade mine, for the world.

But not all my childhood memories were so positive. Which might be why it became so important to me to give my own daughter the perfect childhood I had never known.

4

Searching for Michelle

At eight-thirty a.m. on Tuesday morning, November 27th, the phone rang again. This time I was awake and grabbing for the phone by the end of the first ring. Surely it would be good news! If not Michelle calling, then someone calling to tell me she was somewhere in some hospital, recovering from an accident or even a wild party, but alive and safe.

My hopes fell when I heard another authoritative male voice depressingly similar to last night's caller. "Hello, is this Michelle Rigg's mum?"

"Yes, this is she. How can I help you?"

"This is Detective Senior Sergeant P* [full name withheld] from Coomera police station. I'm in charge of investigating your daughter's disappearance."

Coomera was the next suburb over from Helensvale. I interrupted the voice on the phone. "Hold on! Did you say 'detective'?"

"That's right."

New dread squeezed at my stomach and lungs. A simple missing person's case would be handled by local constables. Detectives were called in only when there was suspicion of foul play.

"I thought this was a missing person's inquiry," I said, trying to keep my voice calm. "Why would detectives be involved? What are you trying to tell me? Where is my daughter? What's going on?"

"I don't know yet, ma'am," Detective Senior Sergeant P* answered soothingly. "But we are treating your daughter's matter seriously. I have every police officer under my command searching for her as well as a helicopter surveilling the area from her home all the way up the Gold Coast to Surfers Paradise. As a precaution, we also have divers searching the nearby canals. You may be aware that this is Schoolies season, so we have more officers allocated to the Gold Coast than we would normally have. We will be using every available officer to help us with your daughter's case. We *will* find her, I promise you. I will keep you informed as the situation unfolds. Is this the best number to contact you?"

"Well, actually, you can reach my husband and me anywhere on our mobiles." I provided both numbers.

I could hear the detective noting them down. Then he suggested, "I think it might be prudent if I passed along any further information to your husband, if that's okay with you. You might find it less stressful."

I knew what he meant was that he wasn't sure how I'd cope with bad news if he had to deliver it over the phone. Since I wasn't sure either, I agreed to his suggestion. I learned later that the police already feared the worst and were trying to spare me from additional heartache. The detective felt that my husband would be able to break any eventual bad news to me more gently.

By this time, I was feeling as though I'd been caught in the climax of some suspense movie where things have suddenly become deadly serious and the protagonist is facing trouble with a capital T. In a movie, all you had to do was wait for the next scene, where the suspense would end and all would turn out happily. But this wasn't a movie. This was the real thing, and there was no guarantee the outcome would be a positive one.

No! I immediately waved that thought away. *They will find her. The detective promised me!*

I was becoming more and more frustrated. I was also beginning to fear the worst as any mother would under these circumstances. Instinctively, I reached for my mobile to call Michelle's number, hoping to convince myself this had all been a bad dream. If I could just hear her voice! But all I got was that same message with the dumb cartoon voice.

Only then did I remember that the police had confiscated Michelle's mobile as well as Adam's in order to track any incoming calls. How could that have possibly slipped my mind?

To keep my mind calm, I tried to push away all the possible scenarios of what could have happened to my daughter. It would be easiest if I tried not to think about the current situation, at least until some concrete information emerged. If I could just find something happier to think about—like the past when Michelle was still my precious little Christmas angel. Or even further back when life still seemed so full of hope and opportunity for the future.

But going back to youthful memories wasn't enough to banish pain and grief. Yes, there had been good times, especially when I was still young enough to be the petted little sister, as least to my two closest brothers. But the good times and camaraderie I've mentioned between the "Three Musketeers" did not totally compensate for a lack of attention or affection from our parents and older siblings. Being the youngest, I was often overlooked, as my parents didn't have the time nor inclination to answer my childish questions or give me the attention I craved.

Even at that young age, I learned quickly that it was best to observe and say nothing until I was asked for an opinion—which wasn't often! Times have changed somewhat, but at that time a father was the undisputed head of his household, and my siblings and me were expected to show respect to him at all times, never talk back or question his orders, and do exactly as we were told or expect consequences.

Of course, life wasn't easy for my parents either. Dad worked long shifts and was only home on weekends. That left Mum to run the house on her own, a huge task with seven children to care for and feed. With Lily and Armando both working, helping Mum with household chores fell to my other two sisters, Lourdes and Gloria, who were next in age.

At first, we "Three Musketeers" were considered too young for regular chores. Once I was old enough, I was expected to do my share. But none of the boys were ever asked to help around the house. In that era and culture, household chores were considered "women's work".

What was far more painful to me as I grew older was that my two nearest brothers stopped welcoming a little sister into all their various games and activities. Of course, I too was changing and, yes, becoming more feminine. I can see now it was perhaps to be expected that my brothers would prefer to spend their time with other boys instead of having a little sister always tagging along. In time, the tomboy who was once happy to play among the bushes and trees with her brothers and their friends metamorphosed into a quiet, sophisticated teenager with a natural flair for fashion, who took pride in her appearance no matter the circumstances.

Unfortunately, the youngest of my three sisters, Gloria was still five full years older than me, so neither she nor the other two had any interest in including me either. My response to being left out by both my sisters and my brothers was to go off on my own, sulking and feeling unloved. In truth, despite the fun I had tagging after my youngest brothers, I have few memories of any kind of love being shown to me. For instance, I don't remember ever being cuddled as a child, either by older siblings or my parents.

It was a sad feeling, and perhaps that lack of love accounts for my own inability as I grew up to express love or show affection to others easily. Including to my own daughter!

Still, growing up in that environment ignited a fire in my belly that made me determined to succeed in life. Let me make clear here that my parents always provided for us as best they could, which wasn't easy with nine mouths to feed. While we didn't have a lot of material things like toys or presents or even a doll to play with when I was a little girl, there was always plenty to eat. Food on the table and clean clothes for her family were my mother's priorities, and I'll always be thankful for that.

One activity we did always do together as a family was to attend Sunday Mass. While Catholicism is no longer Portugal's official religion, as it was until the early 1900s, the majority of Portuguese still consider themselves Catholic, including my entire extended family. So my earliest memories include attending Mass and listening to the priest's weekly sermon. Since the Mass was in Latin, I understood little. But the priest's sermons emphasized fearing God and the punishments God meted out for sins if they were not properly confessed and atoned for. So I grew up afraid of God.

When I felt convicted of sin, I would go to confession and tell the priest what naughty things I'd done since my last visit. He would give me a few Hail Marys or other prayers to recite and pronounce my sins forgiven. Even as a young child, that never felt right. It seemed there must be something more that was needed to earn God's forgiveness than simply reciting a few rote prayers.

My parents also performed the rosary with us children every night. For those not familiar with the custom, a rosary is a crucifix attached to a string of beads, each of which correlates to a specific prayer, whether the Lord's Prayer, Hail Mary, the Apostles Creed, and others. Each night before bed, we would all kneel in the living-room, reciting together the various prayers. Since these were all memorized, reciting them became a very mechanical process. Speaking to God in our own words or asking God for help or advice as though he were a friend or loving Father was not a concept we were ever taught.

In truth, by the time I was school age, I found going to Mass and reciting rote prayers every evening quite boring. At church, my mind would drift to other topics far more interesting to me than Latin words I barely understood. Still, I was afraid of God. Even more so, I was scared to death of going to hell if I did something wrong. So my spiritual and religious life throughout my growing-up years consisted more of begging God for forgiveness and living in fear of his punishment than any concept of loving God or that God loved me.

During these same years, life was difficult for our entire family. We dearly missed the extended family we'd left back in Portugal. For us children, we especially missed our grandparents because of the love and security we associated with them. Dad was saving hard, putting aside every penny he could to repay the massive debt back in Portugal.

This didn't leave much of his income to spend on seven children and a wife. It hurt to attend school year in and year out without many of the things other children took for granted, such as new clothes, new shoes, new school bags, etc. As the youngest girl, I had to be content with hand-me-downs that had already gone through three older sisters.

This might all seem pretty minor, but not for me, since being a foreigner already made blending in more difficult. Having to learn a new language left me struggling with my studies. As with my older siblings, I felt unloved and rejected by my teachers and other students. So began the "why me" syndrome that was to follow me for a very long time.

Nevertheless, we all had to adjust to this new life that was so very different to the one we had left in Portugal. Dad eventually quit his job in Paris and went to work for the new Renault Factory in Sandouville, Seine Maritime, not far from Le Havre in Normandie. My oldest brother Armando also got a job there, and they travelled to work together. My oldest sister Lily found employment in a textile company, where she remained until her retirement.

By 1970, we were living a little more comfortably and settled into life in France. Lily and Armando were now both married while my second-oldest sister Lourdes had graduated from college and secured a well-paid job with the police department. My sister Gloria was working as a TV technician, while my other brothers, Tony and John, attended a technical college, learning mechanical skills that would allow them to join my father and Armando at the Renault factory. I was in my senior year of high school and looking forward to attending university.

Around this time, friends of my parents, a Portuguese family who lived in the next block of apartments, immigrated to a country then unknown to us—Australia. They and other immigrants referred to Australia as the "lucky country" and "land of plenty". My Mum was now struggling with health issues, and both my parents longed to return to a warmer climate as well as a better life, so these descriptions captured their interest.

It was eventually decided that my parents and their four youngest children—Gloria, my two youngest brothers Tony and John, and myself—would immigrate to the city of Sydney, which was the capital of the state of New South Wales on the southeastern coast of Australia. Since Lily and Armando were married and well established in France and Lourdes had a promising career ahead of her in the police department, my three oldest siblings chose to remain in France.

Before I knew it, the wheels were in motion, and I was embarking on the greatest adventure to date of my life.

5

Mystery, but for One!

Though these last terrible hours were not the kind of adventure I'd ever envisioned when I left France for a new continent and home!

I told Stephen how I'd just tried to call Michelle. What was wrong with my normally clear-thinking, intelligent brain that I couldn't manage to wrap my mind around the most basic of details? But Stephen didn't seem surprised at all.

"It's perfectly natural for your mind to play tricks because you so desperately want Michelle to answer the phone," he reassured me. "I am just thankful the police are taking this so seriously. You know, I have a couple of business appointments in Oxenford tomorrow morning. When I'm done, why don't I go over to Michelle's house and see what I can find out for you?"

Oxenford was another suburb near Helensvale, where Michelle's duplex was located. I seized gratefully on Stephen's suggestion. "That's a great idea! It certainly can't hurt, and at least we will know what's going on!"

As promised, the next morning Stephen drove over to Michelle's home as soon as he'd finished his business calls. He could hardly believe his eyes. There were police cars everywhere. The police department had erected a tent on her front lawn as a mobile command center from which to conduct their inquiries and investigation. Dozens of police crews and volunteers from the State Emergency Service were combing bushland, forest, and waterways near Michelle's home.

The media were there in droves as well, waiting with anticipation for any new information to broadcast. Good or bad, it didn't matter since the grimmer the news the more viewers it would attract. To me throughout that horrible time period, the media crews and their vans and cameras and caterpillar mikes felt like a flock of hungry vultures just waiting for their prey!

Maneuvering his vehicle up Michelle's driveway, Stephen pulled up beside the tent. He was immediately approached by a man who introduced himself as Inspector H*, chief of the Gold Coast Criminal Investigation Branch (CIB). When the inspector discovered Stephen's identity, he quickly ushered my husband into the tent where he would be out of range of the media cameras.

Stephen learned that the police were treating Michelle's disappearance as a homicide. They believed harm had come to my daughter and had a suspect in mind. But they couldn't reveal the suspect's identity as they were still conducting their inquiries, which included interviewing anyone who knew her, including friends and family members, work colleagues, and ex-boyfriends.

Conversely, when the police spoke with me or made statements to the public, they projected a very positive outlook, saying that they believed Michelle could still walk through the door at any given time. "You would be surprised how many times we've seen this happen," they'd assure me. "You mustn't lose hope, Mrs. Fox. We'll find her!"

There was no doubt in my mind that their reassuring statements were just smoke screens. Still, I wasn't going to give up, so I kept on praying that my daughter would be safe and return home soon. But even though I wanted with all my heart to believe this would happen, my common-sense inner voice kept telling me, "I don't like your chances!"

5 | Mystery, but for One!

When I learned from Stephen just how extensive the search for Michelle had become, it felt as though I'd been cast without my consent into a horror movie. Stretching out on the couch in the living-room, I tried to watch TV as a distraction to my fear and worry. But my thoughts just kept churning.

What I am doing here? I don't want to be in this. It's too scary, and I want out right now! I want my life back like it was before this nightmare. All I ever wanted was to call my daughter and invite her to dinner so we could plan her birthday party together.

Again, my thoughts drifted back to the events that had led to my beautiful daughter's Christmas birth. While these were not all good memories, they had brought to me the most precious gift I could ever have envisioned, and for that even the painful memories were worth it.

* * *

My parents, siblings, and I arrived in Sydney, Australia, in February 1971. Though I had turned eighteen years old a month earlier, I was still a minor by French law (where the age of majority was twenty-one), so I wasn't really given a choice about going. But like the rest of my family, I quickly fell in love with this magnificent country that was my new home. It was as sunny and beautiful and plentiful as we'd been told.

Still, however much I came to love Australia, moving to yet another foreign land was intimidating for an eighteen-year-old, and I battled major culture shock. Once again, there was the language barrier, not to mention blending in with a whole new set of peers. Here we go again!

Fortunately, our Portuguese friends, who were by now well-established in Sydney, had done all the necessary legwork prior to our arrival. They found us a house rental that came with furniture and appliances so we could move in immediately. They also acted as translators for job interviews. They were a God-send to us those first couple years until our own family became fluent enough in English to handle such tasks.

For my part, having already learned one new language at such an early age had given me an aptitude for languages, and English had been one of my favourite subjects at school back in France. Unfortunately, I wasn't fluent enough upon arrival to pick up where I'd left off in the French school system. As common in the northern hemisphere, French schools ran from September to June while south of the equator in Australia they ran from February to November. This meant that I'd almost finished my senior year back in France but would have to repeat it from the beginning in Sydney since we'd arrived in February.

Our Portuguese friends tried to enroll me at the school their daughters attended. But it had been one thing to adjust to a new school system in a new language at age six. For the level of studies Year 12 entailed, the language barrier was just too much to ignore. Since Australia has compulsory school attendance only to age seventeen, I opted out of redoing my senior year. But neither did I have the qualifications or language skills needed to go straight on to university in the Australian system.

Instead, I decided to "find myself" by job hunting. My sister Gloria had already found employment as a technician at W.D. & H.O. Wills, one of the world's largest importers and manufacturers of tobacco products, based in the UK but with auxiliary holdings in Australia. The department where Gloria worked did tobacco packing, and I asked her to put in a good word for me. She did, and I was given a job.

Packing loose tobacco was piece work, which meant the harder I worked the more I got paid. But I quickly determined this job wasn't for me, so I asked my supervisor to keep an eye out for a vacancy in the administration division. I'd learned to type at school in France, and just a few days later I was offered a job as typist. For me this too was just a start as I had no intention of remaining there long-term. As

5 | Mystery, but for One!

I became more confident with my English, I applied for a position at Sydney's Attorney General department and was offered an opening in the Births, Deaths, and Marriages (BD&M) section.

By the mid-seventies, our entire family was feeling at home in this new country. My siblings had all settled into jobs they liked, and life was looking good. My mother didn't venture out to join the workforce but enjoyed staying home and just being Mum. In consequence, she never mastered the English language like the rest of us. But that never bothered Mum since there was always one of us happy to act as her interpreter when she needed to communicate with someone.

In time, we met other immigrants from France as well as other Portuguese families in the area. My parents had by now managed to pay off the farm debt, but Australia had become our home, so we never did move back to work the farm. Instead, it was kept as a holiday home, and family members still enjoy travelling there for vacations in the beautiful Portuguese countryside.

Without the cloud of debt, my parents were able to purchase a comfortable three-bedroom home in the eastern suburbs of Sydney near the beach. This involved a sizeable mortgage, but with four grown and employed children living at home, the mortgage was quickly paid off as my siblings and I contributed from our wages. I loved my new life in Australia and specifically our new family home on the ocean. My siblings and I were making new friends and having fun.

But not all of life was rosy.

6

Turning Back Time

By the time we emigrated to Australia, my parents, siblings, and I had stopped saying the rosary together as a family. After all, we were now adults and often not together in the evenings. But we still attended Mass together every Sunday because my father had a very strict policy. If we lived under his roof, we abided by his rules and did what we were told—regardless of how old we were.

I didn't mind going to Mass with the family. But Dad was very strict in other ways as well, especially with me as his youngest daughter. One time not long after we'd moved to Australia, Dad took it upon himself to follow me from work to see if I was coming straight home as he'd ordered me. That day was payday, when it was customary for people to go shopping after work or out on the town with their friends. I'd informed Mum of my intentions to do some shopping after I picked up my pay cheque. So when I arrived home later in the evening, I was stunned at my father's anger.

"Where were you?" he demanded furiously. "What were you doing? Where did you go?"

Since I was an adult now, I felt I should be able to make my own choices. It also didn't seem fair that my brothers could go out and do what they wanted, while he kept a constant watch on my activities and was reluctant to let me go anywhere with my friends. When I turned twenty-one, I thought things would change since I was no longer a minor. But no, I still needed a chaperone whenever I went out.

I recognize now that Dad was just trying to protect me, and it was part of his culture to be more protective and strict with daughters than sons. But the constant restrictions and surveillance left me rebellious to the point where I just wanted to get away from my father's oversight and be a free agent, doing whatever I chose to do like other adults.

I can admit now that it was in part just to get away from home that I began dating a good-looking young man named R* with enough charm and gift of gab that I fell for his attentions. We were married when I was twenty-three years old. Like me, R* was from a Portuguese family and had been raised Catholic. But he had no interest in church or God, so once we were married, I quit attending church as well. I still prayed, though, on my own, confessing my sins and reciting the rosary prayers, hoping this would be enough to keep me in God's good graces.

R* was an accomplished chef who had been trained in England, and though his profession necessitated working long evening shifts, he earned a good wage. But his salary alone wasn't enough for a young married couple to live well, much less purchase our own home. So we decided that I would keep working until we could save money for a house.

This also meant we would need to delay starting our own family. Especially since we hadn't been married long before I learned that R* was less interested in saving for a house than in purchasing luxury items we couldn't afford. We ended up moving from one place to another because we couldn't afford the rent with R*'s spending habits.

Unfortunately for our plans, I discovered just two years into our marriage that I was pregnant. R* didn't take the news well at all since this meant I would have to stop work at least for the normal maternity leave any female employee received when they were pregnant. Even once I returned to work, we would need to hire a babysitter, not to mention all the other expenses of a baby.

R* insisted we couldn't afford a baby so early in our marriage. Still, I was shocked when he went on to suggest we would be wise to terminate the pregnancy. Like me, he had been brought up in the Catholic church, which taught that abortion was a terrible sin, so I couldn't understand him suggesting this. He was furious when I responded with an emphatic "NO!"

A few weeks later, almost three months into my pregnancy, I was feeling unwell. Expressing concern, R* offered to take me to the hospital to check that all was okay with our unborn child. At least that's where I thought he was taking me. Instead, R* drove me to an abortion clinic.

Being young and naïve, I thought he'd just taken me to a different hospital somewhere in the city. It wasn't until a nurse came in to prepare me for the procedure that I learned what was about to happen. I was horrified. Getting dressed as quickly as I could, I ran out of the abortion clinic and took the bus home. I don't know what R* thought when he found out I'd left, but he eventually realized I wasn't coming back and took off on his own.

Following that incident, R* became increasingly violent and verbally abusive towards me. When he came to the point of actually hitting me, I knew I had to leave. After all, if my husband could physically lift a hand against his pregnant wife, he would undoubtedly do it again.

We didn't have a phone, so I ran downstairs from our apartment and across the street to a petrol station, where I called my father. Dad drove over immediately, bringing my two brothers, Tony and John, with him. The four of us went back to the apartment so I could collect a few belongings to take with me to Mum and Dad's house until we sorted this mess out.

This was one time when I appreciated having an overly-protective father and big brothers. When R* opened the door, my father had heated words with him, ordering him to stay away from me and never, ever raise his hand to me again—or else! His actual threats were far stronger than that. With three strong male family members now backing me up, R* looked scared and immediately apologized for his lack of control and selfishness. I then left for my parent's house, determined to give birth to my child with or without R*.

If there is one lesson I eventually learned from all this, it is how much babies feel their mother's emotions, good or bad, even while still in the womb. I have no doubt my poor little unborn daughter felt everything that occurred that day. Did this contribute to her own later rebelliousness?

If so, who could blame her! I do remember vividly a heart-to-heart moment years later when she informed me bluntly that if she had the misfortune to encounter her biological father, who hadn't visited her since she was six months old, she wouldn't hesitate to smack him across the face for all he'd put me through. That never did happen—either seeing R* again or smacking him.

Returning to my story, I finally gave birth in December 1978 to a beautiful baby girl, whom I named **Michelle Amanda**. I was so happy when I heard the doctor's announcement: "It's a girl!" After all, this precious baby daughter was my little princess. She was going to be the doll I'd never had. My living doll.

Michelle was such a blessing to me. I always thought of her as being a gift from God. God's Christmas present to me, in fact, since she was born in December, so I often referred to her as my Christmas baby. That God would give me such an angel to care for, even after I'd stopped going to church, was to me a sign that God wasn't just a stern disciplinarian ready to pounce when I sinned, but someone kind and loving who really cared about me.

Michelle was such a gorgeous baby that anywhere we went people would comment on her looks. Of course, nothing could have made me prouder. I was on Cloud Nine. Please forgive me if I am being repetitive, but as you can see, I simply adored my little girl. She was mine, all mine, and no one was going to take her away from me ever!

* * *

I was roused from my memories with a jolt, jerking upright on the living-room couch. In my attempts to distract my anxious thoughts, I must have drifted off to sleep because I suddenly found myself staring at my daughter. Not the sweet newborn infant I had just been cradling in my heart and mind, but the adult woman whose beautiful features had held so much anger the last time we'd seen each other.

Right now, none of that mattered. I would rejoice to hold my Christmas angel in a mother's embrace again, no matter what she said or did.

Then I recovered full consciousness enough to realize it was not Michelle I was staring at, but a photograph of her being broadcast on the TV, which I'd turned on before sitting down on the couch. I reached for my spectacles so I could see more clearly, then sat staring at the TV screen, my eyes wide-open in shock, as the prime-time news anchor finished an update about Michelle's disappearance and asked cooperation from the public in finding her.

This is just a bad dream, I told myself. *It can't be real. I just need to go wash my face, splash some cold water over it, and wake up for goodness' sake!*

I did just that. But since I was already awake, it didn't change anything. Nor did it help to turn the TV to a different channel. When a mother sees her daughter's face plastered across four separate prime-time news programs, she knows it's bad. That isn't some nebulous stranger being talked about, but her child!

I cannot describe how I felt when I finally came to grips with the reality that it was Michelle being discussed on that TV screen, Michelle whose fate the police were expressing concern about. This was no bad dream, nor a scene from a fictional horror movie I was playing a part in, nor some other alternative my mind was trying to trick me into accepting. This nightmare was real, very real!

What made matters worse was that my own job history had made me only too well aware of the statistics on situations like this. An overwhelming majority of such prolonged disappearances turned out to be homicides, and reality was telling me I was foolish to be expecting anything else for my own daughter.

Still, I tried to maintain a positive faith. Michelle would turn up unharmed because everyone was praying for her. God had shown himself real to me, not just through the birth of my Christmas angel, but under far more difficult circumstances in the following years. Besides, the loving heavenly Father I had come to know and trust wouldn't let anything happen to my daughter. After all, she was still young and had a bright and prosperous future ahead of her. Any moment now, the phone would ring to give me the good news that the police had found her as they'd promised me they would.

The phone did ring. And find her they did. But I should have remembered that God's ways are not always our ways, nor are his answers to our prayers always what we expect.

7

Overcoming the Odds!

Part of my confidence that God could still turn this nightmare around was because I had witnessed him do so repeatedly over the years since Michelle's birth. And not because I deserved it. It was only God's great grace, mercy, and unconditional love that kept my life from flying completely off the rails even when I was going my own way and making the worst of life choices.

Beginning from Michelle's earliest years. After her birth, life changed for me big time. Even before she was born, R* was already pleading with me to take him back. He promised to change and that he would never lay a finger on me or the baby. My family tried to talk me out of this. But I wanted my baby to grow up in a stable environment with both parents there to care for her, so just a few weeks before Michelle's birth I ended up going back to my husband.

This turned out to be a poor decision on my part. R* had rented a new apartment for the three of us in an upmarket suburb of Sydney, Bellevue Hill. When he began arriving home later and later into the night, I assumed this was due to his responsibilities as head chef. I didn't learn that he was having an affair until the woman called me at home, looking for him.

Then one night when Michelle was just six months old, R* didn't

7 | Overcoming the Odds!

come home at all. Worried that he'd been in some accident, I called the police. There was no such report of anyone by that name being in an accident. Instead, I found out that R* had been arrested for an incident of disturbing the peace at a nearby nightclub. I learned later from my brother John, who freelanced as a DJ at that nightclub, that he'd seen R* there with various women when I'd thought he was at work.

I never did find out the details of the incident. But after a night in jail, R* was released and came home. For me that was the last straw. I applied for divorce as well as full custody, both of which I received. Meanwhile, R* was by now being hounded by debt collectors and chose to disappear from Sydney as well as my life. Not once did he contact me to see his daughter, and he never did pay a penny of child support,

Even though I put on a brave face, it wasn't easy bringing up a child without her father. With my usual attitude of determination, I would tell Michelle, "We're going to make it, baby girl. We'll be fine, you'll see." Then I would remind myself, "It's better to be alone than in bad company!"

Being a stay-at-home mother was not an option since I was paying board at my parents' home and had other expenses for Michelle and me. So I went back to work at BD&M. I also secured additional weekend work as a receptionist at the Marriage Registry. All this meant that I had to rely on my parents to take care of Michelle while I was working.

The long hours took a toll on me, and I found that by the end of the day I had no time or energy for cuddles with Michelle. Wasn't that ironic? I was too busy making ends meet to show affection to my gorgeous little baby, just as my parents had been when I was young. History has a strange way of repeating itself, as I found out.

This scenario went on for four years. Too long for my liking, as it was hardly an ideal arrangement as far as I was concerned. But I couldn't afford to live elsewhere, especially with a young child. Besides, my daughter needed to feel safe and loved. And that she certainly did. My family couldn't have loved her more. In fact, they spoilt her rotten.

The problem was that I as her mother had no parental authority over Michelle whatsoever. I couldn't discipline her when I thought it necessary because her grandparents would come immediately to her rescue, saying, "Poor little mite, leave her alone!" In consequence, Michelle came to see me more as a big sister than her mum and my parents as her mummy and daddy instead of her grandparents.

The situation was extremely frustrating, and I knew I needed to do something about it. But there was nothing I really could do since I had nowhere else to go. Then one Saturday I was working overtime at the Marriage Registry. While I stood there waiting to usher in the scheduled wedding party, a charismatic, athletic man with an unmistakable English accent introduced himself to me as Jack Rigg. I found out later that he was a successful criminal solicitor. The very next week, he asked me out on a date.

Jack was fourteen years older than me, but we quickly developed a close relationship. To my delight, he had a wonderful way with children, and Michelle felt very comfortable with him. Since she had no recollection of her biological father, she soon started calling Jack "Dad". He didn't have the heart to correct her, and in any case, he soon became "Dad" officially when he asked me to marry him.

This new situation was working well for all three of us. We were quite a happy little family, and Jack treated Michelle as lovingly as though she were his own biological daughter. **In** fact, it wasn't long before he adopted her legally, at which point her last name also became **Rigg**.

Nor were there financial worries anymore, since Jack's profession as a criminal solicitor paid well. I was now enjoying luxurious vacations, dinner parties, going out to nice restaurants, flowers, jewelry and more. Wow, what bliss!

7 | Overcoming the Odds!

Jack also believed I had it in me to do better in life, so after our wedding he encouraged me to enroll in a secretarial course at the Sydney Metropolitan Business College. Taking a twelve-month leave of absence from BD&M, I completed the course, excelling in shorthand. I was extremely happy about this as my ultimate goal was to become a court reporter, which necessitated good shorthand skills. Instead of returning to BD&M, I accepted a job at the Department of Public Prosecution, or DPP. This was followed by a secretarial position at the Sydney Law Courts Library.

It wasn't just my life that was going well. All of my family members who had come to Australia were happy to make this beautiful country the last stop as our home. We had all become Australian citizens and settled in. We all had jobs that provided a good living for our family. My sister Gloria had married and had a daughter named A*. My closest brother in age, John, married three times, and out of those marriages came his children N* and A*.

Our other brother Tony never did marry, but with Michelle my parents now had four wonderful grandchildren here in Australia along with those back in France. These included Armando's two daughters, K* and M*, while Lourdes had a son and daughter, E* and P*, giving my parents a total of eight grandchildren. We occasionally visited our siblings who had remained in France and their families as well as our extended family in Portugal, sometimes travelling all together as a family and other times just with our own spouses. Even though we lived on separate continents, our family always remained closely connected.

In all this time, I had continued to pray to God on my own whenever I needed help. Since Michelle's birth, I'd begun to think of God as a friend and would talk to him about my problems and situation. After I married Jack, I started attending Sunday Mass again as well. Jack had been raised Church of England and didn't attend church. But I began taking Michelle with me because I wanted to introduce her to God.

Still, I found myself daydreaming through the monotony of the Mass ritual, and attending it didn't really make me feel better. I felt I needed something more, but I had no idea where to find it.

Then once again, my bubble of happiness burst. Jack and I had been married only five years when I discovered that my new husband, who had brought so much joy and harmony to our household, was also cheating on me. Even though he routinely described me to others as a beautiful and dedicated lady, it seemed he couldn't be happy with just one woman. He wanted more.

But he also wanted Michelle and me. Jack arranged to move out on his own, telling me that he needed his freedom. But he didn't immediately ask for a divorce, insisting he still loved Michelle and me both and wanted to be part of our lives.

Well! You can't have your cake and eat it too, right? Eventually, our separation and, later, our divorce became official. But it took a long time because Jack was reluctant to let go, and he did remain in our lives to a certain extent since he still considered Michelle his daughter and to Michelle he was still her daddy.

For my part, I couldn't believe what was happening. Here Michelle and I were again on our own and having to fend for ourselves. It seemed that the moral of my story so far was to never feel too comfortable in any given situation because it could blow up in your face at any time!

One positive development by this time, if nothing else, was that Michelle now understood that I was her mother and my parents were her grandparents. But my separation from Jack was a major blow for a nine-year-old little girl trying to understand why the only daddy she'd ever known had left us.

Sadly, Michelle quickly turned the situation to her advantage by manipulating both of us to get what she wanted. This worked like a charm for her since Jack felt guilty about his actions so he rarely denied her anything, while I felt caught in the middle of it all, like meat in a sandwich, and frightened to lose my daughter's love. On my salary, I couldn't provide her with all the things she demanded, which gave Jack the upper hand in competing for her love, since he could afford to buy her anything she asked for.

Once again, as when she was being raised by my parents, I was losing any parental authority I had over my daughter. I finally had to concede that the whole scenario was too difficult for me. In fact, it became unbearable. When Jack and I were a couple, we had decided to place Michelle in private school, since nothing was too good for our little girl. After the divorce, Jack continued to pay half the tuition, but even the remaining fees and other costs were far more than I could handle, so I had to get a second job to cover my share.

In consequence, I was once again working very long hours with a lot travelling, which in turn left me exhausted and with little time to spend with Michelle. My daughter had also become accustomed to a very comfortable lifestyle with Jack, and she didn't understand why it couldn't stay the same after Daddy left. Even with two jobs, I couldn't afford to keep up "appearances" the way she expected. She even started asking me to drop her at the back of the school so the other kids wouldn't see the second-hand car I was now driving.

All of this put me under enormous pressure, financially as well as emotionally. I began feeling as though I was somehow responsible for what had happened to us. That this was all my fault because I hadn't been "good enough" to keep Jack from seeking out other women.

Still, I kept going because I didn't want Michelle to undergo the turmoil of being pulled from her school or deprived of the upscale lifestyle enjoyed by the other students. After all, I'd known as a child how it felt to stand out from the other students because I couldn't afford the nice clothing and other things they had.

What a mess! Once again, the cry of "why me" was ringing its bell in my head. I was devastated, but the only thing left for me to do was to keep my head high as best I could, trying not to let it show.

8

Unveiling the Past

To Michelle's credit at such a young age, she did her best to understand our situation, and she seemed happy enough with the new arrangement of seeing "Daddy" every second weekend. But as her mummy, I should have realized she needed extra love and attention. Unfortunately, I again failed to provide her with that comforting security blanket. I was simply too busy working to have time or energy for any of this. The result was that my poor little darling felt unwanted and unloved, though I didn't see it then.

Over the following years, I continued working long hours. I also went out occasionally with friends or on dates. After all, I was only in my mid-thirties, and I'd have gone insane without the occasional reminder that life shouldn't be just work and no play.

I made a point too of taking Michelle to Sunday Mass with Mum and Dad whenever I could, usually every two weeks since I worked every other weekend. But this was more for moral support and company than any sincere seeking after God. Above all because I felt like a hypocrite every time I walked into church with my parents. I knew they weren't happy with my life choices or the men I was dating. And I was even more sure God didn't approve of my current lifestyle.

Then in my own longing for love and attention, I made the worst mistake of my life, a decision I would always regret. Yet I give thanks to God for his great mercy and forgiveness because he used that terrible mistake to draw me to himself. I had finally given in to a relationship with a man who had been pursuing me for quite some time. Soon after, I found myself pregnant.

I was stunned and frantic, especially since my "boyfriend" had no interest in marriage or raising a child. As a single mum, I was barely managing to support one child. And I knew my parents, who had been there for me through two divorces and raising Michelle, would be furious if I had a child out of wedlock. And what would Michelle say, since she was already reaching her teens?

Instead of praying about the decision, I went to a close confidant who knew my situation and asked for advice. The advice I received was to terminate the pregnancy. When R* had suggested an abortion, I had been shocked, vehemently refusing to even consider such a terrible sin. For which I will always be grateful, as that decision gave me my beautiful daughter.

But this time I listened to my fears and persuaded myself it wasn't really wrong. After all, only a very small percent of Australians still opposed abortion, including church-goers. Even fewer in my own age group. I went ahead and had the procedure, telling myself I was making the most rational, sensible choice. But afterwards, I felt wracked with guilt.

I wanted to confess to my parents but was even more afraid of how they would react than over telling them I was pregnant. After all, in the eyes of the Catholic church, abortion was a *big* sin. All my life I'd lived in fear of God's punishment. Now I had committed a sin that seemed beyond forgiveness. I couldn't even go to Confession to receive absolution for my sins, since that would mean revealing my secret to the priest. Talk about a hidden thorn!

My only real hope was to convince myself that the religion I'd grown up with was just fables and myths, as so many of my friends believed, because that meant there really wasn't a God to punish me. But that option offered me no comfort either, so I lived with a constant feeling of guilt and regret.

Then one day I met one of my parents' neighbours, a Portuguese lady named Maria who for years had been inviting my parents to visit her church. One weekend they finally accepted her invitation. When they told me they would be visiting Maria's church, I was curious enough to ride along with them.

Wow! All I can say is that I was blown away by the experience. The worship music made me feel alive, and the people were friendly and welcoming. Best of all, the pastor preached powerfully straight out of the Bible. The congregation also carried well-read Bibles instead of a missal, the liturgical book of responsive readings and prayers we had always used for Mass.

My parents were equally impacted, and before long, we were attending services there regularly. Through the pastor's teaching, I learned that we serve a forgiving God. The devil will always try to convince us otherwise, if we let him. My sin was huge, perhaps the biggest sin of which a woman could be guilty. But God intervened, dying on the cross in the Person of Jesus Christ to save fallen humanity from their sins—and that included even me!

I also came to understand that it was not confessing to a priest or performing a series of Hail Marys or some other assigned penance that brought about forgiveness of sin, but that I could go straight to God in prayer. If I confessed my sins to God and repented from the depths of my heart, God would not only forgive me, but grant me eternal life in his Kingdom. That's good news in any language, right? What more could a sinner want?

Having carried my inner demons around for so long, I couldn't believe the answer had been in front of me all this time. As I watched others go forward during altar calls to confess their sins and ask Jesus into their heart, my own heart was filled with longing to do the same.

Jesus tells us in Scripture, "The truth will set you free" (John 8:32). And I knew that I had to confess my "hidden thorn" and repent with all my heart, or I would be doomed forever.

Thankfully, I was also learning that we serve a loving God. I'd grown up hearing about Jesus Christ dying on the cross. But for the first time I understood that God was not just interested in punishing us for our sins. Scripture tells us:

> God so loved the world that he gave his one and only
> Son, that whoever believes in him shall not perish but
> have eternal life. (John 3:16)

Just knowing God cared about me that much was the most indescribable feeling. In fact, from the moment I found out that the God I'd thought was so angry with me for being a sinner actually loved me so much that he gave up his only Son to save me, I was dizzy with happiness. In return, all God asked of me was to welcome him into my heart as my Lord and Saviour, be baptized in his Holy Spirit, and enjoy eternal life with him in heaven forever.

On a cold, windy Sunday morning during the winter of 1994 in Bondi Beach, Sydney, I did just that. I gave my life to Jesus and surrendered my heart to him as my Lord and Saviour. That day was without a doubt the best day of my life, even more so than the Christmas birth of my daughter.

9

Facing Reality

If it were not for that day I gave my life to Jesus, if not for the assurance of a loving heavenly Father and the comfort of God's Spirit, I could never have made it through the week following Michelle's disappearance. Bad news travels fast, and by now both our in-country family (Mum, Gloria, and Tony) and my siblings in France (Lily, Armando, and Lourdes) had become aware of the situation. As a result, I was inundated with phone calls left, right, and center.

In addition, Senior Detective Sergeant P* was calling Stephen with daily updates as he'd promised, which Stephen would then recount to me. By this juncture, the detectives had made clear they suspected Michelle was a victim of foul play. It also seemed evident that Adam was their prime suspect. Neighbours reported hearing Michelle screaming at Adam and vice versa around the time Adam claimed they'd been fighting Friday evening. Nor had any of the neighbours seen Michelle leave the house on her alleged walk.

Later, one of those same neighbours apologized to me for not having called the police when she heard the shouting. Unfortunately, people are reluctant to call law enforcement in domestic violence incidents because they don't want to get involved. Please, dear reader, if you ever find yourself in such a situation and suspect domestic abuse,

9 | Facing the Reality

have the courage to at least call a crime-stoppers tip line. You might save a life!

But despite their suspicions, the police didn't have enough evidence to charge Adam. We found out later that they had placed him under surveillance and were watching him around the clock. They were also upping the pressure on him, bringing him in for multiple interrogations in the hope that he would crack under the stress and confess. But so far, they had not caught him in any suspicious activity. Nor did Adam waver from his original story, reaffirming his love for Michelle and insisting that he would never hurt her.

By now, the police had also been through Michelle's contacts list on her mobile, interviewing and re-interviewing all potential suspects. This included the male friend with whom Michelle had planned to attend a yacht party the evening of her disappearance. He insisted he had not seen her that evening. Nor had she answered her phone or let him know why she had bailed on the party. It had, in fact, been the worries of various friends like him who had known Michelle's plans that led to her being reported missing when she didn't show up at any of her scheduled social events.

In any case, the friend proved to have a solid alibi for the time of Michelle's disappearance. And by the time the detectives finished going through the rest of her contacts, they expressed confidence that all had accounted for their whereabouts or had no reason to be considered as suspects. None were held for further questioning.

The volunteer search of the forests and wetlands around Michelle's neighbourhood had also been suspended. It had become clear to the police that, whatever had happened to my daughter, she was not anywhere within a "cooling off" walking distance of her home. Either someone had picked her up at some point during her walk and taken her elsewhere. Or she had returned from her walk and left again elsewhere.

Or she had never gone on a walk, as Adam had testified, in the first place.

A two-day in-depth search of Michelle's home as well as the yard had yielded no clues either. Over time, we learned what the police had found in their search—and hadn't found. Her purse and car keys remained missing, but her car was still there, so if she had returned and then left again, someone else had done the driving.

The only physical evidence of significance had been a pair of muddy shoes in a plastic bag they'd found dumped in the garbage disposal wheelie. These were precisely Adam's size, and the plastic bag had his finger prints on it. But unless some foul play could be attached to the shoes or mud, there was nothing criminal about throwing away a pair of shoes.

One other piece of evidence seemed more than incriminating to me at least. This was a text message among the angry interchanges between Michelle and Adam the police had found on their mobiles. The text in question had been written by Adam to Michelle:

```
I don't hate you. I am at the end
of my string. I'm about to crash in
a big way. I had thoughts of doen
[misspelled] things 2 you that aren't
good so best if I leave.
```

Of course, Adam dismissed this as simply part of a typical couple's argument. It could even be taken as proof that he still cared about Michelle and was trying to defuse the situation by offering to move out. With no body to substantiate foul play, there was nothing the police could do to disprove his version of their exchange.

It had now been a full week since Michelle had last been seen, so of course the media outlets were hungry for news. They could smell a story and were naturally keen to hear from the police. The police

9 | Facing the Reality

in turn needed the public's help to assist them in their inquiries if they were to have any hope of finding Michelle, so they suggested that Stephen and I work together with the media to make a televised appeal for information.

We agreed. When Stephen and I arrived at the Gold Coast Police Media Center, where the press conference was being held, I became overwhelmed by the jostling crowd of reporters and multiplicity of cameras and microphones lined up right in front of us. Panicking, I burst into tears, unable to utter a word.

Immediately, Stephen stepped forward and took over. The noise and confusion didn't faze him as he had dealt with the media often over the past decades. In fact, his father had been the general manager of Channel 10, one of Australia's major commercial television networks, and Stephen had worked for another television network, Channel Nine, before going into business for himself, so he handled the rest of the press conference with no hesitation.

I, in contrast, was an emotional wreck. Not just during the press conference but afterwards when it became clear no one in the millions who had listened to our appeal was going to come forward with any new information to help us find my daughter. I couldn't understand why this was happening. Why God was letting this happen.

Especially now of all times when after long years of mother-daughter conflict, of wrong choices that had left Michelle's life an even greater train wreck than my own, my daughter had finally turned her life around. I had truly believed the worst was over and there was a glimpse of light at the end of the tunnel.

And Adam had played a major part in that transformation. How was it possible the man who had brought so much joy, hope, and stability to my daughter's chaotic life was now prime suspect in her disappearance?

10

New Beginnings

I spent far too much of my life blaming myself for Michelle's problems and for her choices. And even though I have come to recognize that my daughter made her own choices, I also know that my own shortcomings and choices played a contributing role in both our lives. Even after giving my heart and life to Jesus Christ, it wasn't always easy to stay on track because the devil was constantly trying to lead me astray, whispering in my ear that I was still a sinner and that I wasn't good enough to be forgiven.

One reminder that helped me was praying each morning before heading out for the day the Lord's Prayer (Matthew 6:9-13), especially those verses that read:

> Forgive us our debts, as we also have forgiven our debtors. And lead us not into temptation, but deliver us from the evil one. For if you forgive other people when they sin against you, your heavenly Father will also forgive you.

"My heavenly Father has forgiven me," I would rebuke Satan. "He will deliver me from you and your temptations."

Each time I stood firm against Satan, my faith grew stronger and stronger. And I needed to be strong because Michelle was now sixteen years old and becoming uncontrollable at home and at school. Much to my horror, my beautiful little princess was turning into an impossible brat. I'd had no control over her for some time, but now she wasn't listening to Jack either. As the nursery rhyme goes, she could be very, very good (with Jack when she wanted something from him), but when she was bad (at home with me), she was horrid!

Michelle had become an expert at lying and devious behaviour, so for a long time neither Jack nor I had any idea of what she was getting into. Blessed with a good brain, she didn't need to study hard to pass exams. She used her smarts instead to do drugs.

Such a lifestyle exposed her to all kinds of bad influences and dangerous situations. But she didn't seem to care, in part because she considered herself smarter than everyone else around her, so she was sure she could escape the consequences of her behaviour. This included hanging around with juvenile delinquents and even bringing them to our apartment when I was at work. The neighbours complained of Michelle and her friends throwing eggs and wild parties.

One time, she was even caught stealing. Instead of demonstrating shame or repentance, she responded insolently to the police, taking for granted that Jack would bail her out of the situation since he was a criminal solicitor. She also stopped caring at all about her studies. In eleventh grade, she finally dropped out of school altogether. I did my best to help her realize she was making a terrible mistake. But she made clear nothing I said had any influence on her.

Just when I felt things couldn't get worse, my father fell very ill. He was diagnosed with cancer and passed away less than a year later in June 1995. I was alone with him in his hospital room when he took his last breath, and his death was a great shock to me and the rest of our family.

This was one time when Michelle, though just sixteen years old, was really there for me as I was for her. She too was devastated at losing Papa, as she called her grandfather, whom she respected and loved immensely. Thank goodness, we still had each other, and we both turned to the other for a shoulder to cry on when we needed to be consoled for our loss.

We carried out my Dad's wishes to be buried in his native land, Portugal, where he had purchased a plot in the family crypt of his old parish's cemetery. All of us siblings were concerned how his death would affect Mum, since they had been married for over fifty years and he was the love of her life. But she showed tremendous strength through it all.

One major blessing was that both my parents as well as my other siblings who were living in Australia had committed their lives to God and trusted in Jesus for salvation not long before Dad was diagnosed with cancer. After his passing, it became very evident that Mum was drawing strength from her faith in our Lord Jesus Christ during this very difficult time in her life.

And God never failed her or any of us in the months and years ahead. Life once more fell into a routine. Tony was still living at home, and Gloria lived just a few houses down the block. My youngest brother, John, lived a good hour away, even further when Sydney's traffic was congested. But he had always made a point of visiting my parents, along with his son, on a regular basis. After Dad's passing, those visits increased to every weekend and sometimes more, his way of keeping an eye on Mum. So though the love of her life was no longer with her, Mum was always surrounded by family.

By this point, I had grown exhausted with working such long hours and wasn't enjoying my position anymore. I'd always had a private dream to work in Beauty Therapy but had been too busy supporting Michelle and me to pursue such an opportunity. Now I decided I really needed a change, so I left my Public Service job and enrolled at the Beauty Academy in Sydney.

After graduation, I went to work for one of Australia's biggest retail stores in Australia, David Jones. But while the glamour of my new profession shone for a while, I soon found that all that glitters is not gold. To make good money, I had to work weekends as that was when retail stores were busiest and paid more for overtime. But I didn't want to go back to that hectic schedule.

Then I came across an ad for the position of office manager/secretary with a small company, Executive Professional Register (EPR), that specialized in writing professional résumés. The job was ideal for my professional experience, and the pay was good. Even better, the position was a normal nine-to-five work schedule, so no more weekend work. I applied and was offered the position. What a welcome change!

Meanwhile, my angel continued to drift away. Michelle was now seventeen years of age and more and more difficult to live with. She wasn't communicating with me at all, and since Jack had minimal fatherly influence over her either, she became more uncontrollable and cunning. I honestly didn't know where or who to turn to. I knew I had to do something to stay sane, but what?

Now that I had surrendered my life and heart to Jesus, I had made a commitment that I would not date just for the sake of companionship. The next man I dated would be for keeps. He would also have to share my Christian faith. But neither did I feel like going out on the town with female friends since this tends to attract men on the prowl. So I stopped going out socially altogether, sticking instead to a much safer environment—the EPR office.

Sure enough, that's where I met Stephen Fox, a businessman who had come in to have his professional résumé written. As secretary, I typed up the résumé and was impressed by all Stephen had achieved in his life thus far. When he picked up the finished document, we had opportunity to converse briefly, and I sensed there was something different about this guy that I couldn't help but admire. It wasn't just that he was handsome and well-dressed. He carried himself with a confident poise and the kind of class money can't buy. I don't know quite how to describe it as it is something you either have or you don't—and he did!

We exchanged phone numbers, and Stephen called me almost immediately. I found out that he too was a follower of Jesus Christ. Stephen had been brought up in the Church of England, but at age thirteen, he had attended Dr. Billy Graham's first crusade in Sydney, Australia, and had raised his hand at the altar call to accept Jesus as his Lord and Saviour. Our faith was something we shared, but there was also a definite physical and emotional attraction on both sides. Still, I was very cautious from the start.

Okay, be very careful here, I told myself. *You don't need to get involved in anything that could get you hurt in the process!*

I made clear to Stephen that I was looking for long-term commitment and if he wasn't interested in that type of relationship, we would both be wasting our time to start dating. To my delight, he was in complete agreement. He also made clear he genuinely wanted to get to know me as well my complex situation. That alone was refreshing and comforting to me. As we began dating, our relationship grew by leaps and bounds.

Michelle, however, didn't approve at all of my relationship with Stephen and was very vocal about it. She still considered Jack her father and didn't like the idea of sharing me with anyone else, so she saw Stephen as a threat. Despite her objections, we were married in February 1996 after a brief courtship. Like me, Stephen had been married before, so neither of us felt we needed a long engagement.

I was also hoping a family environment would settle Michelle down as it had when Jack and I were first married. Not that I expected Stephen to take Jack's place in Michelle's life, but I did hope she would be happy for me and look up to Stephen for advice.

Sadly, she instead rebelled totally against us. Michelle and I had been living on our own for the past eight years, and in her mind she was losing control of her mum to someone she barely knew. She displayed her aggravation by staying out all night and getting involved

10 | New Beginnings

repeatedly with the wrong people.

Stephen in turn had never had to deal with anyone like Michelle before. Along with her general rebelliousness and bad language, she refused to take any advice or orders that came from him. I found myself constantly stuck in the middle, feeling pushed to choose between my husband and my daughter. All of which put an unbearable stress on our new marriage.

Michelle turned eighteen, an adult in the Australian system, just a few months after our marriage. By then I'd recognized that our best solution was for her to move into her own place, giving Stephen and me the peace we desperately needed as newly-weds. I found a studio apartment close enough that I could keep an eye on my daughter while she in turn could be independent.

Once I'd set it up with all the necessities, Michelle moved in. She was in her element having her own place and living as she wanted. More importantly, peace was restored to our home and marriage. A win-win situation for both parties.

At least it seemed so until, her current boyfriend moved in with her. He was using drugs, a huge concern. He also rarely worked, so he would push Michelle to call me and plead for yet one more handout to pay for electricity, groceries, etc. He would also take her possessions to trade for drugs, including a small diamond that had been a gift from me to my daughter. Unfortunately, since Michelle was now legally an adult, she was free to do whatever she pleased.

In the middle of all this, Stephen told me that he was feeling God's leading to move back to Queensland, the state just north of New South Wales, where he had previously had a very successful business practice. Wanting to be a good wife, I gave my support to the move. But I wasn't happy with the decision. Sydney had been my home town since my family arrived there from France, and it had never crossed my mind that remarrying might mean moving away from my family and daughter.

Bottom line, I didn't like change—at least not this kind of change. Why? In truth, the little girl in me just didn't want to leave her mother. I had never lived more than a short drive from my parents, and I'm not ashamed to admit I still needed my Mum, especially now that Dad was gone. It was as simple as that!

Still, I was now married, and I loved my husband, so I felt I had no other choice but to follow Stephen to a new home in what is called Australia's Gold Coast more than eight hundred kilometres from Sydney. But though I had submitted to my husband's wish, I was hurting inside, and regret slowly built up over being separated from my daughter.

The one thing that comforted me was knowing that my family was close by to keep an eye on Michelle and protect her if necessary. And they did just that until she decided to follow me to Queensland just a few months after our own move. Unfortunately, she brought her drug-popping boyfriend with her. Since Michelle had a family who cared about her and were willing to help her financially, he was happy to tag along and live off her.

Bad move, baby girl!

11

A Different World

Another name for Queensland is "the Sunshine State", and a TV ad that still occasionally runs here to promote tourism brags, "Great one day, perfect the next!" While I found the Gold Coast sunnier than Sydney, I must say I never really warmed up to it. With my Mum, three siblings, and my daughter living in another state, I felt quite the opposite—cold, unloved, and lonely.

I did occasionally fly back to Sydney when my longing for my Mum and my siblings became too much for me. It also helped when Michelle moved to Queensland. Deep down, I think her biggest motivation was that she too needed and missed her Mum.

But though she was much closer to us now than Sydney, I still didn't see her often. She had settled with her boyfriend in the Sunshine Coast, a heavily-populated area about a hundred kilometres north of Brisbane, the state capital. The Gold Coast was almost seventy kilometres south of Brisbane. Michelle and her boyfriend were living basically on government dole (welfare cheques) and family handouts along with occasional odd jobs like fruit-picking. Not the life I had envisioned for my bright, talented little girl. But at least she was alive and well, and I was grateful for that.

Soon after our arrival in the Gold Coast, I went back to my earlier profession as a beauty therapist, renting a room at a nearby hairdressing salon, which allowed me to work back and forth from home with minimal travel. I soon had a successful practice. With Michelle close enough to visit and work I enjoyed, life looked promising, and I was happy again. All I needed now was to find a good church.

I did find a wonderful Bible-centered church, and Stephen began attending there with me, at first reluctantly since though he had accepted Christ as a teenager at the Billy Graham crusade, his sporadic attendance of Mass in the Church of England had been as rote and perfunctory as mine in the Catholic church. But he was as blown away as I had once been at the difference in worship and in-depth Bible teaching at our new church. Now he too really understood for the first time what giving his life and heart to Jesus was all about.

This encounter with God completely turned Stephen's life upside down. Like a child who has been deprived of food, he just couldn't get enough of Jesus. He not only attended church with me but read and studied anything about Jesus he could get his hands on. Not just the Bible but Christian books and Bible study material. He wanted to know more and more about this wonderful, kind divine Being who willingly sacrificed his life on the cross to give sinners like us eternal life.

Stephen was so happy in his new-found relationship with Christ that he wanted to share it with everyone—especially Michelle. Like me when I was growing up, Michelle knew *about* Jesus, as I had taken her off and on to Mass as a child. But she didn't know him personally and intimately. Ever since my family and I had surrendered our hearts and lives to God, we had never stopped praying that Michelle too would one day ask Jesus to live in her heart.

So I was very happy when Stephen bought my daughter a special "beginners" Bible that was in modern English, easier to understand and more appealing for a teenager to start reading. Michelle had mellowed toward Stephen enough to accept the gift graciously. But

11 | A Different World

that was the end of it. We never broached the subject again, and I had no idea if she was actually reading his gift.

I hadn't seen Michelle for quite some time as with my work schedule I couldn't travel almost two hundred kilometres north to visit her on a regular basis. But I'd given her my mobile phone number, assuring her she could call me anytime if she needed anything. I'd also told her about my beauty practice and its location in relation to where Stephen and I lived.

Then one day out of the blue, Michelle contacted me at my beauty therapist practice. She told me she and her boyfriend were now staying with his parents in Brisbane, but she was looking for a place on the Gold Coast to be closer to me. Wow! It made me so happy that she wanted to be near me. She then asked if she could come see me at work.

"Sure!" I said immediately. "When?"

"Right now," she responded. "We're at the café next door, sitting outside."

"Great! I'm coming right out," I said.

I walked out to the café, but I almost froze in my tracks with shock when I spotted my daughter with her boyfriend. She was so thin she looked anorexic. He was just about as thin. I ordered coffee and cake for both of them, guessing they didn't have any spare cash. They devoured the food as though they hadn't eaten in days.

I couldn't stay long as I had a client waiting for me at reception, so I asked Michelle if she could come back later. She refused, saying they both had to get back to Brisbane and had just dropped by to say hello. But before they left, Michelle put her hand out in the cupping gesture that is a request for money, the look in her eyes pleading, *Please help me, Mum!*

I couldn't ignore my daughter's plea, so I opened my wallet. I don't normally carry much cash, and most of my clients pay by credit card, so all I had was a single fifty-dollar note. Giving it to her with a hug, I whispered in her ear, "Come back to the salon, and I'll treat you to a facial and a hair treatment. You look like you need a bit of pampering."

With a nod, she followed her boyfriend down the street. I stood there for what seemed an eternity, watching the two emaciated figures walking away. All I could think of was how weak and frightened my sweet daughter looked. Tears filled my eyes, but I quickly shook them away, composed myself, and went inside to tend to my client, who was still waiting at reception.

After my client left, I immediately phoned Jack. Even though we were divorced and I had remarried, we had always remained on good terms because of Michelle. Jack still loved his daughter dearly and had never ceased to care for her in a fatherly way, a quality I admired in him and for which I was grateful.

When I described what I'd seen just minutes earlier, Jack was not surprised as he'd been concerned about Michelle's condition for some time. He told me that he'd spoken to her a few times lately and even tried to convince her to move back to Sydney, where he could keep an eye on her. But his fatherly advice had been like water off a duck's back. She just didn't want to hear it.

Hearing this was devastating to me because the only person who'd been able to get through to Michelle in recent years was Jack. If she wouldn't listen to him, I didn't like her chances. Suddenly, her future was looking extremely grim.

I'll never forget that pitiful sight of my little girl, once so pretty and happy and now looking completely miserable and wasting away to nothing. I realized then that what I had witnessed was an accurate picture of what can happen when a young couple gets hooked on the poison of drugs, each dragging the other along for the ride. It becomes virtually impossible to turn away and stay clean, unless you can break away completely from that other person who is pulling you down. If anyone reading this thinks otherwise, take a moment to ponder what

11 | A Different World

I'm saying because you are fooling yourself. Drugs can kill, and sticking to a partner who has no interest in getting clean might just cost you your own life!!

God alone knows how many times Jack and I tried to reach out to Michelle and failed. But we never gave up on our little girl, and neither should anyone on their loved ones. Jesus tells us in Scripture, "Seek and you shall find" (Matthew 7:7). And indeed, help is sometimes just around the corner disguised as a stranger, and it will find you before it's too late if you will just seek it. There's hope out there for all of us.

12

The Unbreakable Bond

I discussed the situation at length with Stephen, and he agreed with me that my daughter desperately needed her Mum right now. We decided that Michelle and I should live together for a period, just the two of us as we had before I married Stephen, so that I might talk some sense into her very troubled mind. This would necessitate me leaving not just my husband, but the comfort and safety of our home, and renting a small apartment nearby for Michelle and me. Our hope was that being together would trigger some spark within her, giving her a feeling of safety and security and reassuring her that I was there for her no matter what.

We gave it a try, but after six months I had to throw in the towel. In truth, I no longer had anything in common with this emaciated, lost young woman who had been my precious little princess. Michelle became violent to the point of threatening me with a knife. This scared me out of my wits, and I finally recognized I had to get out for my own safety. She was undoubtedly suffering from drug withdrawal symptoms, and I wasn't mentally equipped nor trained to deal with it.

I returned home with Stephen, and we found Michelle a small apartment in a nearby suburb of the Gold Coast. She liked the new arrangement, especially since I was paying her rent, and seemed to settle down, much to my relief. But it wasn't long before I began receiving phone calls from her landlord, threatening to evict my daughter if she didn't start behaving. We found out that he had been receiving numerous complaints about noise, parties, people coming and going, etc., at Michelle's unit.

Then we learned that her same druggie boyfriend was back in Michelle's life and had all but moved in with her. He had also brought the dog they'd owned together, Tyson, a "staffy", or more specifically a Staffordshire Bull Terrier, a breed related to pit bulls, but much gentler and less aggressive. I objected less to the dog, who could at least offer Michelle some protection, than to her boyfriend, who contributed nothing. By now I was fuming. This had to stop!

Calling my daughter, I told her firmly, "Michelle, I've had enough of this. I've had a chat with the landlord, and I've decided that I cannot continue to pay the rent for you and your lazy boyfriend, whom I don't recall inviting to live in a place I'm paying for! If I keep paying your way, you will never learn how to stand on your own two feet. From now on, you're on your own!"

Michelle responded with such abusive language there was only one thing left for me do, and that was to withdraw from the whole situation. It wasn't an easy step to take, but I knew I had to be true to my word. In truth, by now I'd gone through much of my savings and could no longer afford to keep paying her rent.

I advised her landlord of my decision. Within a few weeks, he called to let me know he had evicted Michelle and her boyfriend for non-payment of rent. With no other option, Michelle finally got her act together enough to find a place of her own. Thankfully, she also responded with more understanding than I'd expected when I explained that I loved her dearly, but no longer had the financial means to pay her way.

"Don't beat yourself up, Mum," she told me. "I've made my choices, and it's not your fault. You've been a great mum, and I love you."

It was a turning point for her and for our relationship. To cover her rent, Michelle began taking in boarders. I was relieved and proud when of her own accord she asked my approval of any new roommate before letting them move in. As for her boyfriend, she finally mustered up the courage to kick him out, though she kept their dog Tyson. She eventually got herself another staffy, a female called Ninja. Michelle loved dogs, and those two were her babies.

My heart prayer was that she would rise above this ugly phase in her young life and begin to thrive. And she did. In the end, it was clear we'd made the right choice in giving Michelle "tough love" because once she realized there'd be no more bailouts and she had to make it by herself, she began turning the sheer determination that had always been part of her character to good use instead of teen rebellion.

Now that a drug addict boyfriend was out of Michelle's life, she completely stopped taking drugs. Despite the years of abusing her body and mind, she had retained her sharp intelligence. She took a job as a sales representative in telecommunications. An extrovert and natural salesperson, she was immediately successful.

Then suddenly a fresh challenge entered our lives. When I married Stephen, our future together had looked promising and rosy. Even with uprooting to Queensland, I had found happiness in my new life, job, and church, especially now that Michelle was nearby. But not long after I moved back home to my husband, Stephen fell ill to the point that he could no longer work. Not a good thing for our plans of a great future in the Sunshine State!

At first, not even his doctor could figure out Stephen's medical condition. For no apparent reason, he would simply crash with a total lack of energy by the middle of each day. Even knowing what a hard-working human being my husband had always been, I myself took some time to recognize that he definitely was unwell. He was finally diagnosed with Chronic Fatigue Syndrome (CFS), a horrible illness that only those affected by it can really understand what it feels like.

Here we go again! I thought to myself. Maybe I wasn't a single mum this time, but with Stephen unable to work, I was once more the sole breadwinner for our family. And since my beauty therapy practice was not enough to support two people, I would need to find a much better-paying job.

One thing different this time around was that I now had my heavenly Father to turn to, and I did just that, asking God to open the doors to the right job. And God answered my prayer, leading me to a position as a sales representative for Pure Water Systems, a company that sold and installed water purification systems. I'd been told many times over the years that I have the gift of gab and could sell ice to the Eskimos. But the proof was in the pudding. Could I really do that? Off to work I went and soon found out that, yes, I could and did!

In my new job, I made it a habit to dedicate my day to the Lord. Each time I got out of my car to go into an appointment, I would ask God for his help and blessing. I should mention here that part of my income as a sales representative was a weekly bonus once I achieved a pre-determined and agreed-to target of sales. I knew I couldn't afford to miss out on that extra bonus because with Stephen's illness and household expenses we needed every dollar. So I worked hard, and every single week I reached my target. Thank you, Jesus!

I felt so blessed! Yes, I was doing my part in working very hard, but I also knew that God was working on my behalf, and one thing I never failed to do at sales meetings every Monday was to give God the glory. Other sales reps would laugh at me for my outspoken faith, but I didn't care because I knew my God always delivered, and I had faith in him.

And sure enough, at the end of my first year I was awarded as that year's "Best Sales Person". Yes, I had earned it in part because of my commitment and hard work. But all I'd really done was honour God above all things, and he in turn blessed me beyond my expectations.

On the negative side, I was once again having to work long hours. My husband needed me due to his health issues. My daughter needed me too. Though she was at least now holding a job and paying her own rent, she was still struggling with leaving the drug scene behind and making a new life for herself. But I was so busy just trying to juggle everything to the best of my ability that by the end of each day, though I knew how important it was, I had little energy left for showing love or sympathy to either of them.

Thankfully, after about two years Stephen began to emerge from this dreadful illness and was able to help me with my job, since he had work experience in sales and was very good at it. As a businessman, he also had the know-how to start his own company, having done it successfully in the past. The New Millennium was now upon us. Like most people, we had our expectations as well as apprehensions of what the future might hold. But one decision Stephen and I made was to take the risk of starting our own business in water purification systems, which we called Perfect Water Systems. We opted to set it up from home to minimize overhead. With Stephen's business expertise and my own experience in sales, this worked very well, and our business venture proved a resounding success.

Praise God, what a relief! I could now take a back seat and let Stephen lead the way, as should have been the case right from the beginning. I had married my husband for better or for worse, and to this point the scales had been tilting more south rather than north. So I was happy to see them change direction. In my opinion, it was about time they stayed tipped towards "better" permanently!

13

A Call to Obedience

Amid this entire situation, something very special happened that is still a warm, bright memory in the midst of those dark, stormy years. Aware that I spoke Portuguese, friends invited us to their church to hear a visiting pastor from Mozambique, a country in southern Africa that was once a Portuguese colony and still spoke Portuguese as their official language. The church was also in the process of planning a two-week mission trip to help with this pastor's ministry in Mozambique.

After the service, Stephen said to me, "I've just had a word from the Lord. I think he wants you to go on this trip."

"Excuse me!" I quickly responded. "I never received any such word! Maybe God was speaking to you. Have you thought of that?"

I resisted in part as I felt he was pushing me because I spoke Portuguese versus any real call from God for me to go. But Stephen continued to encourage me to volunteer, and I decided to accept the challenge.

If I can help in a small way by being there, why not do it? I told myself. *After all, what could possibly go wrong?*

To my delight, two young women from the church, one in her late twenties, the other in her late teens, also volunteered. It was all shaping up to be an exciting adventure. Then shortly before our scheduled departure, my two teammates ran into a problem with the compulsory vaccinations and had to reschedule to a flight several days after mine.

I was devastated, as I had a fear of flying, especially alone and to a country I had never been before. But I boarded the plane on my own, totally trusting in God. The plane stopped at Perth, the capital of Western Australia, to refuel and take on more passengers. The next stage was to Pretoria, South Africa.

I was getting more and more anxious about the flight ahead when another woman took the seat next to me. She clearly sensed my discomfort because she took my hand as the plane headed down the runway and whispered to me, "Don't worry, dear! It's going to be all right."

At her kind words, my fear dissipated. We chatted most of the way, and when we touched down safely in Pretoria, I silently thanked God for his protection and for sending that kind lady to comfort me. A few days later, my two teammates turned up, and we flew on to Beira, Mozambique's fourth largest city right on the coast across from the island nation of Madagascar.

This time our flight was on a small prop-plane. If I'd been frightened in a jumbo jet, I didn't think I could possibly cope in this toy-like little plane. The two young women with me could sense my fear, so they tried to cheer me up by making jokes all through what seemed the longest flight of my life.

When we arrived in Mozambique, I was stunned at what I saw. The country was just emerging from fifteen years of civil war, and much of the infrastructure had been destroyed. All around, we could see buildings in ruins and abandoned. We'd been briefed about what to expect, but I'd never dreamed it would be quite this bad.

The Australian missionary in charge of the compound that would be our home for the next two weeks met us at the airport. Piling into a truck, we all sat in silence as we drove past heartbreaking sights on

13 | A Call to Obedience

all sides. Never had I felt so rich and privileged as I did during my time there, and adjusting to the living conditions was certainly not easy, especially the lack of sanitation and general stench. But despite the poverty and destruction, everyone we met seemed to manage a welcoming smile for us.

Two things in particular left an imprint in my heart while I was there. One of our assignments involved visiting local homes, which were nothing more than mud huts, to pray individually with the residents. Being fluent in Portuguese, I didn't need an interpreter, so the young Australian lady in charge of our group accompanied my two fellow volunteers, while I went on alone.

Knocking on the door of a hut, I found a lady waiting for me with a couple of friends who also needed prayer. The woman shared several ailments that were troubling her, after which I proceeded to pray for her. I then did the same for her friends.

By the time I'd finished, my hostess was so overwhelmed with emotion that she started crying. I had brought along some pretty handkerchiefs with the intent of giving them away, so I handed her one to wipe away her tears. Her face lit up with a big smile, though tears still rolled down her cheeks. She just couldn't believe I wanted her to keep the handkerchief. When I insisted, she turned around to pick up a huge pink shell prominently displayed on a shelf.

Handing it to me, she said, "I want you to have this."

I was stunned, especially since I could see how little she had in that tiny, one-room hut. I quickly replied, "No, no, thank you so much, but no, I cannot take this. The Australian customs won't let me through the airport with this big shell in my luggage."

"Please, you have been so kind to me and my friends," she insisted. "I know it is not much, but this shell is special. My husband found it when he was diving for fish. I want you to have it as a token of my appreciation for your prayers and your beautiful handkerchief."

I could see she would be deeply hurt if I didn't accept her gift.

Needless to say, I took the shell. When I did go through Customs back in Australia, I explained with great innocence that it was a gift from a little lady in Beira, Mozambique, where I'd just been on my very first mission trip. God was interceding for me that day because the Customs inspector let me keep the shell without any drama. I found just the right place for it in my home, where it remains to this day as a reminder of generosity and kindness from someone who greatly touched my heart.

The second memorable event happened one Sunday when we attended a local church where the Mozambique pastor we'd met in Australia was preaching. My fellow volunteers and I sang some worship songs in English, which received enthusiastic applause. Then the pastor stood up and introduced me as a Portuguese-speaking missionary. As everyone clapped, he turned to me and said, "You've got the floor. Here's a Bible. You're preaching."

What?!! I couldn't believe what I'd just heard. I spoke Portuguese because my mother had thought it important that I never forget my native tongue. But it was not a language I had ever spoken beyond a child's vocabulary or studied in at school, much less read the Bible in that language. Talk about being thrown into the deep end!

But I didn't have long to worry as all the clapping was urging me to get on with it. I still don't know how it happened, but I opened that Portuguese Bible and began speaking. I can't even remember what I said, but I could feel God's Spirit giving me the words. When I was done, I looked over at the pastor and said, "Okay, over to you now. Or do you think they would want me to pray for them?"

"Yes, I think they would," he responded. "So you better start praying!"

Again, I felt completely out of my comfort zone. It was one thing to pray with a few people in their homes, another for an entire congregation. Overwhelmed and not wanting to let these people down, I panicked for just a minute or two. Then a wave of energy and sheer

13 | A Call to Obedience

determination came over me, and I started to pray for them, one after another, the words pouring from me in fluent Portuguese.

After that unforgettable experience, it was time to fly home. My two teammates flew with me only as far as South Africa, where they were staying on a while longer. So once again, I had to fly on my own. While a little disappointed, I no longer found the flight at all frightening, but enjoyable. I was also eager to see my husband and daughter again, as I'd been gone almost a month by now. Arriving at Sydney International Airport, I had to hurry to make my connecting flight to Queensland.

Settling in my designated seat, I noticed that the young man sitting next to me looked tense and anxious. Leaning forward, he closed his eyes and clenched his fists. These were signs of anxiety with which I was only too familiar, and I found myself saying the exact same words that kind lady had said to me on the way to Africa. "Don't worry, dear! It's going to be all right."

Opening his eyes, the young man tried to relax, but he was still trembling. Then he whispered, "I just want it to be over! I want the plane to land and know I'm safely on the ground."

To calm him, I quietly shared my own story of flying to Africa just a few weeks earlier and how terrified I'd been. I explained that I'd been on a mission trip, and this had been God's way of teaching me to place my trust in him by putting me in a situation where I had no other choice but to trust in God and God alone.

"Something happened," I finished, "because I now have no fear of flying at all. It's gone, praise God!"

The young man listened in silence, then muttered "Okay, let's do this! It's going to be all right!"

When we landed, he immediately regained his composure. Bidding him farewell, I went home. Being able to comfort someone else in their time of need made me feel this trip I'd hesitated to take had been totally worth it. In the end, the entire trip was a wonderful experience of learning to trust God in all things.

I could not have dreamed then how desperately I would need that lesson not so far into the future.

14

Adam's Confession

After this most significant trip that will always have a special place in my heart, I quickly settled back into my daily routine. Life was good. And much to my delight, things weren't just going well for Stephen and me. They were also improving for Michelle, who was now in her early twenties. She landed an excellent position with Telstra, Australia's largest mobile phone and Internet provider. Her bosses thought the world of her. With a good job, she was able to purchase a brand-new car and put a sizeable deposit on her first home. I couldn't have been a prouder—and more relieved—Mum. Well done, baby girl!

With the drugs and all Michelle's other problems behind her, it felt as though I was watching a flower blossom for the first time. Sunshine had replaced the cloudy skies, and now at last, my precious daughter was experiencing the sheer pleasure and beauty of being alive. As I watched this transformation taking place, I was downright giddy with happiness. I could hardly believe we had actually made it through this horrible phase of our lives.

By her twenty-eighth birthday, Michelle had completely turned her life around for the better. But she was still in and out of one relationship after another. This concerned me a bit because she'd been through so much and I was longing for her to find happiness with someone nice who would love and protect her, maybe even have children of her own.

When I brought up the subject, Michelle would just shrug her shoulders and say, "I don't want to get married and have kids. I have my dogs. They're my babies. But when I do meet the right person for me, you'll be the first one to know."

To my delight, it wasn't long after our discussion that Michelle called to tell me, "Guess what, Mum! I met this guy last night. His name is Adam Cartledge, and we really hit it off! We're going to see each other again next weekend."

I was happy for her, of course. I would have liked to know more about this new man in her life, but I'd learned by now I'd just have to wait until Michelle was ready to fill in the blanks. She had been dating Adam for several months when she decided completely of her own volition that it was time for Stephen and me to meet the man who was bringing so much happiness into her life. One afternoon without any forewarning, she dropped by our house with him.

Our first impressions of Adam were good. Just under two metres tall, muscled and handsome, he was certainly by outward appearance the type of man who would attract any woman. He was also calm and well-spoken, seemingly the perfect foil to my outgoing, bubbly daughter. If I had a criticism, it was the tattoos that covered his arms and legs. But that was his business, and I really didn't care so long as he treated my precious little girl well.

He was also gainfully employed, unlike Michelle's last long-term boyfriend. His job as a maintenance worker at a convenience store was less prestigious or remunerative as Michelle's booming career as a "solutions specialist" with Telstra. But neither seemed to mind the discrepancy. More pertinently, they both seemed completely besotted with each other. In fact, I had never seen my daughter so happy. If for nothing else, I could be truly grateful to Adam for that.

14 | Adam's Confession

It wasn't long before Adam moved into Michelle's new home with her. They often came over for meals when time permitted, so he was quickly becoming part of our family. It took some time before they reciprocated our hospitality because Michelle wanted her new home to be perfect before entertaining us there. When she was finally ready, she invited Stephen and me over for a barbecue.

The minute we arrived, Michelle insisted on giving me the royal tour. My little princess had finally found her prince, and now she was happily showing off the castle they shared. She was clearly proud of all she'd done with the house and wanting to impress me. I in turn was very impressed and so proud of her achievements.

After the tour, Michelle and I stepped outside to admire her garden. What followed deeply touched my heart. Like a little girl showing Mummy her new drawing, she asked me, "So what do you think? Do you like it?"

Did I like it?!! I was bursting at the seams with joy and pride. Tears came to my eyes as I told her so. Michelle rewarded me with her biggest, brightest smile, just as she'd done when she was a little girl. It was a smile I hadn't seen for a very long time, and I felt I was in heaven right then. It was a moment of sweet, pure bliss I would never forget.

I went on to assure Michelle that not many people had achieved as much as she had in such a short time, especially coming out of the dark world of drugs. She gave me another broad smile and said, "Thanks, Mum! I told you I would make you proud."

With that, she went inside to check on what Adam and Stephen were doing. I stayed on in the garden to savour the moment and contemplate her comments. A wave of pride in my sweet daughter again swept over me. When Michelle returned a few minutes later, I smiled at her and repeated my earlier praise. "Well done, baby girl! I knew you could do it, and I am so proud of you!"

We gave each other one of those mother-daughter "super hugs", then went in to join our menfolk. The moment we'd just shared left me with a new and far more hopeful outlook on my daughter's world and life. The promise of a new beginning for Michelle was looking very exciting.

God is good, all the time! I thought to myself.

For the rest of the afternoon, we all thoroughly enjoyed the barbecue, the new home Michelle had worked so hard to beautify, and each other's company. I could never have dreamed it would be the last afternoon we would all share together. Or that this sunshiny, peaceful new season of my life was about to be swept away by the worst tribulation I had experienced yet.

Of which Michelle's disappearance would only be a terrible last straw. If I could go back to that afternoon with what I know now, how many things would I have done differently over the following months? If I had, would my daughter still be with me today?

Maybe not. But at least love and happiness would have been my final memory of our relationship as mother and daughter.

Though the awful disagreement we would both take to the grave was one thing for which I couldn't lay the blame on Adam Cartledge.

* * *

Eleven long days had now passed since Michelle's disappearance. Everyone including the police kept comforting me, telling me not to give up and to be strong. But after working for years with the DPP and Law Courts Library as well as being married previously to a criminal defense lawyer, I was well aware there was rarely a positive outcome in cases like this. Deep down in my heart of hearts, I guess I knew it was all but over.

Meanwhile, the police had returned to interrogate Adam. Since parts of his account just didn't add up, they had by now made clear that they didn't believe him. As they persisted with their questioning, the cracks in his story began to widen. Finally, on Sunday afternoon,

14 | Adam's Confession

December 2, 2007, nine days after Michelle's disappearance and six days after she was reported missing, Adam was formally arrested. The next day he appeared in the Southport Magistrates Court, where he was charged with my daughter's murder.

That Monday evening, after Adam's court appearance, Stephen and I eventually went to bed. But we tossed and turned for hours, sleep beyond us both. Sometime between three and four a.m. Tuesday morning, Stephen could see I was still awake. Taking my hand, he said, "Let's pray and ask God to reveal to us where Michelle is."

So we did just that, holding hands in prayer. Minutes passed in the stillness of the night before we both started talking together as one, sharing what God was giving to each of us. God revealed to Stephen a vision of tall trees located in a forest and to me a very wet undergrowth.

Considering the revelation we'd both experienced, Stephen and I were now expecting the worst. When morning finally came and the detective senior sergeant called as he always did with an update, Stephen immediately said to him, "This time I have something for you for a change."

He proceeded to share the revelation we had received from God. The officer was very respectful and interested in what Stephen had shared. Later that morning, Stephen felt impelled in his own spirit to go back to Michelle's place. He walked around the property, observing what had been done to her backyard, where the police had dug multiple holes in the hope of recovering Michelle's body. As he walked, he sensed strongly in his spirit that something dreadful had happened there.

Stephen was leaving the property when he encountered a CIB (Criminal Investigation Branch) detective, who recognized him from the televised press conference. As they began to talk, Stephen told the detective, "I sense it in my spirit that something horrible happened here."

The detective just nodded silently, again showing great respect towards what Stephen had shared. What both these law enforcement officials must have thought later, I cannot imagine because within twenty-four hours the truth of what God had revealed to us was publicly confirmed.

Adam was being held at the Southport Watchhouse, which is the facility where prisoners are held while awaiting trial. It was early Wednesday morning when Adam asked the staff to contact Detective Senior Sergeant P., requesting a meeting with him. Upon the detective's arrival, Adam confessed to murdering Michelle by strangulation on Friday evening, November 23rd, which was the evening before Australia's general elections.

I cannot put into words the impact that news had on me. I could only hope and pray that once more Adam had shown himself a liar and that his confession was as false as his protestations of love for my daughter.

If not, then God had not answered my desperate prayers and all hope for my daughter's return was gone. More so, all hope for reconciliation with my precious beautiful Christmas angel, the love of my life, was gone.

Once again, I was left to ask myself in anguished despair, how had I ever let it get to this point?

15

The Senseless Feud

"Forgive your enemies, but never forget their names."
—John F. Kennedy, 1917-1963,
former President of the United States of America.

Looking back, that last awful quarrel that separated my daughter and me seems so trivial, so pointless. But I must also state honestly that it did not seem so then. At the time, I believed I was making the right choice in my actions as well as my reactions. I still am not sure what I could or should have done that would have resolved the situation differently. I will let you make your own decision once you know the whole story.

As I share this painful part of my story, let me state from the beginning that the topic of forgiveness plays a major role in the chain of events to come. So let me just ask, what really is forgiveness? How do we truly forgive? Just saying the words "I forgive you" comes easily enough. But letting go of the internal pain and anger over an offense is another matter, unless you are willing to turn the matter over to God and give him control of your situation.

I can almost hear you say, "That's easier said than done!"

I couldn't agree more. A common proverb tells us to "forgive and forget." But there simply is no way to just forgive without effort and pain, while to go further and actually *forget* what the offender has done or said is practically impossible. We may be quick to advise others against holding a grudge even while we are silently holding on to a grudge ourselves. We may not even realize we are holding on to unforgiveness, since living in denial about our true feelings is quite normal.

Besides, we may feel, why shouldn't we hold on to those feelings? If we are not in the wrong, why should we have to forgive *or* forget? No way! Why should an offender get away with their offense? No, that's not the way it works! They should be made to pay for the hurt and pain they've inflicted upon us.

Or at least that is a way of thinking only too common in our world. We live in "an eye for an eye" world that too often leaves no room for forgiveness. Which is sad because, unfortunately, our world holds plenty of room for error—our own errors as well as other people's. If we don't forgive and forget other people's errors, we can't expect them to forgive or forget ours. As I shared in an earlier chapter, Jesus states this unambiguously in the Lord's Prayer:

> And forgive us our debts, as we also have forgiven our debtors… For if you forgive other people when they sin against you, your heavenly Father will also forgive you. But if you do not forgive others their sins, your Father will not forgive your sins. (Matthew 6:12, 14-15)

Again, this is easy to say, but much harder to do. I had been a believer in our Lord Jesus Christ for many years by now, in fact since 1994. But I still had to learn this lesson the hard way. The experiences I was about to face would change my life. I am so thankful I had my

15 | The Senseless Feud

faith in my loving heavenly Father, the presence of Jesus Christ always with me, and God's Holy Spirit indwelling me, or I never would have survived those experiences, much less had it within me to forgive.

As to forgetting, that I never will. But I don't see anywhere in Scripture where we are told to forget the pain and tragedy that happens to us. Much less our dear loved ones we have lost. Only to forgive the offender.

This part of the story actually starts a few years earlier with my brother John. As the two youngest and only a year apart in age, we'd always had a special bond. We remained close even as adults, and he was still the fun-loving one of the family, always clowning around, enjoying life, and very energetic.

About the very same period when Stephen and I were struggling with his Chronic Fatigue Syndrome, John too began showing symptoms of extreme fatigue. At first, we attributed it to his job as that involved a lot of travelling. After lots of nagging from the whole family, John finally agreed to go in for a medical checkup. Sure enough, there was a reason for his extreme fatigue, and this time it wasn't CFS but cancer.

The entire family was distraught at the news, but for me personally, I was devastated as John wasn't just my brother but dearest friend, and I couldn't accept that my cheeky, funny, energetic fellow "musketeer" had a terminal disease. Over the next six years, our family stood by him in constant prayer, hoping and waiting for a miracle. But God had his own plans and timing for John's life.

In May 2007, I received word that my brother didn't have long to live, so I immediately booked the earliest flight possible to Sydney, hoping to get there in time to visit him in the hospital. Michelle had made plans to visit her uncle before his sudden downturn, so she was already booked on a flight that same afternoon. The earliest flight I could find didn't leave until 8 p.m. As I stood in line to board the aircraft, I pulled out my phone to turn it off in preparation for takeoff.

That was when I saw a text message from my nephew A*, letting me know that his dad had lost his fight with cancer. John had only just turned fifty-six.

A wave of dizziness swept over me, and I almost fainted. I had reached the gate by then, and the flight attendant was asking me for my boarding pass, but I heard only a roaring in my ears. All I could think about was that my brother was dead and my hope of seeing him alive one last time was gone.

Somehow, I made it to my assigned seat. I knew that no amount of crying was going to bring my brother back. But I just couldn't contain the tears, and I continued to weep all the way to Sydney. When I finally reached the hospital, I was greeted by Michelle, who had arrived there only a few minutes before I did.

By now it was late evening. But the nurses had been told that two family members would be arriving from out of town and were kind enough to not to move John until we could say our goodbyes. It felt surreal to see my brother lying so still and lifeless there in the hospital bed. The expression on his face was not one of suffering, but smiling and peaceful as if saying to me, "About time you got here, sis! I'm ready to go!"

The funeral date was set. I helped with arrangements, getting necessary things done but in a robotic way because I felt completely numb and my mind was elsewhere. Unfortunately, in the midst of all this, Michelle was not being easy to deal with, saying unkind things and refusing to control her tongue or temper to the point that I really let her get under my skin.

In truth, I was so preoccupied with the various tasks at hand and with my own grief, I couldn't see that she too was hurting so very, very much. John was not only her uncle, but her godfather, and she had always adored him. So when she lashed out at me, I should have recognized her grief and tried to console her.

Instead, I too was feeling hurt and vulnerable, so I lashed right back. From there, it escalated into a full-blown argument. We were

15 | The Senseless Feud

standing in a hall corridor, and as we yelled at each other, my Mum came down the corridor. She immediately joined in, and what had been a heated, foolish two-way argument now became a three-way yelling match. This really concerned me because at eighty-seven years old Mum had a heart condition, and with her grief over losing her son, I was afraid all this quarrelling might trigger cardiac arrest.

Still, I have always regretted what I said and did next. Swinging around on my daughter, I blurted out words I will never, ever forget. "Stop it, Michelle! Can't you see you're upsetting Gigi?"

Gigi, was Michelle's version of Grandma she'd called my Mum this since she learned to talk. Angrily, I went on, "Why don't you get out of here and go back home? You always seem to cause trouble. What's wrong with you? Show some respect! I never want to see you again as long as I live. Just go!'

16

A Double Whammy

A word of advice to all my readers: be very careful of what you speak out because your words will come back and bite you as they did me. As soon as those hurtful words left my lips, I wished I could take them back. I clapped my hand over my mouth. But it was too late. No matter how sorry I was, the words could not be unsaid nor unheard by my daughter.

Michelle was already storming off. Mum went after her, trying to calm her down. I headed to my room, where I burst into tears. In the end, Michelle didn't leave but stayed for the funeral service. We treated each other civilly for everyone's sake, but I never did get a chance to speak to her alone or say how sorry I was.

At the funeral, we had both been asked to read a Scripture passage, one following the other. Michelle looked beautiful as she read, and I was so proud of her. Despite the tension between us, there was still plenty of love to give each other a heartfelt hug, sealed with a kiss on the cheek, once we'd finished reading.

That hug and kiss will always stay in my heart because it proved to be the last time I would ever be face to face with my wonderful, precious, beautiful baby girl, whom I loved so very much. I would have done and said things very differently if I'd had an inkling this was my

16 | A Double Whammy

last opportunity to enjoy the privilege of being in her presence. As it was, that hug was a moment I have tucked away in a special place in my heart, to be cherished always and never ever forgotten.

After the funeral, John's wife E* made arrangements to have his body flown back to Portugal, as my brother's dying wish was to be buried alongside Dad in the family crypt. Now it was time for me to return to the Gold Coast. But even once I was home with Stephen, all I could think about was the funeral, that terrible argument with Michelle, and how miserable I felt. I just couldn't get my head around the reality that my beautiful brother was gone forever. I will always miss you, John, always!

Thankfully, I had a gorgeous Collie dog named Mr. Biscuits, a wedding present from Stephen back in 1996. If you've had a devoted canine companion, you know how special that relationship can be, sometimes more devoted, loving, and supportive than any human companion. That was what Mr. Biscuits was to me. He was my canine "little boy", since I'd never had a son of my own, and I loved him to bits. When he was cuddled up to me, listening patiently to my outpouring of grief and pain into his furry ears, I was able to find some measure of comfort and peace.

But that wasn't to last long. Within a short time after my return from the funeral, Mr. Biscuits fell suddenly ill with a fast-spreading virus. The virus not only caused a number of serious complications, but also left our sweet little dog in a lot of pain. There were no viable treatment options, and we could not let him continue to suffer pain. So just three weeks after my brother's death, Stephen and I had to make the difficult decision to let Mr. Biscuits go.

I had not expected to miss that little dog as much as I did, and Stephen felt much the same. For weeks, it would take only a glance around the house, and something that reminded us of Mr. Biscuits would trigger our tears. We'd actually had another Collie, Shadow, who was Stephen's dog before we met and had passed away two years earlier. While we'd both felt that loss too, Mr. Biscuits had been special to me in particular since Stephen gave him to me as a wedding gift, so I felt his loss more.

What happened next is another memory I hold close to my heart. Michelle and I were still not on speaking terms, but someone in the family had let her know about Mr. Biscuits, whom Michelle too had always loved dearly. One day after work, she drove over to our home. We were out of town for a few days, so I missed the opportunity to see her. But she left a parcel for me.

In the parcel were two roses, one red and one yellow. Along with the roses was a note from Michelle that read, "The yellow rose is for Uncle John and the red one is for Mr. Biscuits. I'm so sorry, Mum. I know you're hurting, but I am too."

If you are familiar with the language of flowers, you will know that a yellow rose symbolizes eternity and a red rose symbolizes love. As I read Michelle's note, my eyes filled up with tears of love and joy. I reread it again and again, kicking myself for not being there when she came. I kept asking myself the obvious: *Why did we have to go away right then? If only I'd known she was coming, I wouldn't have gone! If only—*

My heart was being torn apart because I so desperately wanted to see her again. My first impulse was to call her and suggest we forget about this stupid feud and start over again yet one more time. Life was too short to let this breach between us continue. At the same time, my pride reminded me that I shouldn't let her get away with her bad behaviour, as she had done countless times before. So I didn't pick up the phone, rationalizing in my own mind that she needed to be taught a lesson.

She can't go on mistreating me the way she does just because I'm her mother! I told myself firmly. *She needs to learn to show me some respect!*

After all, I'd been taught growing up to treat my parents with respect, and I'd done my best to teach her. There was no excuse for her attitude and words of disrespect towards me, and if I didn't stand my

16 | A Double Whammy

ground, she'd never learn. As far as I was concerned, that was the end of the story, and I was not going to change my mind any time soon.

A few weeks passed. Then one particular Sunday after the worship service, I was standing outside chatting with a member of our congregation I knew fairly well. I'd mentioned the recent passing of Mr. Biscuits and how miserable I'd been feeling about it.

The lady was already aware of John's passing, so she responded with immediate sympathy, "Oh, you poor darling, you've sure had a rough time lately. First your brother and now your dog. How horrible! Come on, let me pray for you!"

As she prayed, I tried to contain my tears. When she finished, I thanked her, then added, "Yes, I'm having a hard time getting over it. Things couldn't get any worse, could they?"

Meaning in my mind that I'd had my share of sorrow and grief, so surely I could count on nothing else bad happening to me, right? Wrong! I can almost hear the devil saying gleefully right then, *You haven't seen anything yet! Just you wait!*

17

Inevitable Guilt

Michelle and I had interacted at John's funeral because grief had taken over, understandably bringing us together. But since that day, sheer stubbornness on both sides had kept the two of us away from each other. Every day I would think of Michelle and how I should go about breaking this long silence between us. When I asked Stephen's advice, he agreed with my own position: "How else is she going to learn if you weaken? She will never respect you!"

I too felt we'd made the right choice. But when I called my mother to ask her opinion, she responded very differently: "You've only got one child, so put your pride aside and call her!"

"But, Mum, I'm sick and tired of letting her walk all over me!" I argued back. "Remember, you were there. You saw how she treated me that day, how she spoke to me. It's time to teach her a lesson. Otherwise she'll never learn. It's now or never!"

At this point Mum broke in softly, "What would Jesus do? Doesn't he teach us to forgive?"

"Yes, Mum," I responded. "But the Bible also tells us to respect our mother and father!"

What a dilemma! My heart was telling me to forgive and forget because life is short and I missed my daughter so much. But I also

17 | Inevitable Guilt

wanted to be treated with respect. Was that so much to ask? For years, I'd put up with her insolence, just letting it slide over and over while Michelle never once apologized or made any effort to change. Mainly because I'd blamed myself for all the turmoil she'd gone through due to my failed marriages. After all, none of this was her fault, so to make up for it, I'd tried to give her whatever she wanted and forgive her anything she did.

The fight at the funeral was not particularly worse than other fights. It just had greater impact because of the timing, right when Michelle knew we were all grieving the loss of my brother. That's why this particular incident was for me the point of no return. I wanted it to stop once and for all!

Even so I was already wavering. I had decided to give the current situation until Michelle's birthday, which was coming up in December. If by then she hadn't reached out to me, I would pick up the phone and invite her out for a birthday celebration at a restaurant of her choice. Then, hopefully, we could both put this stupid, worthless feud behind us.

Bottom line, all I wanted was to be a family again. To start afresh, so to speak. We had a lot of mother-daughter catching up to do without wasting precious time being stubborn. And the truth was that I needed my daughter badly to help me cope. I was still struggling with a big void in my life at the loss of my brother, who had been so close to me. My heart was broken, and I didn't know how to mend it.

Nor could I turn for comfort and cuddles to my loving, devoted Mr. Biscuits. Talking to my canine "son" about my loss had been the one thing that helped me feel better. As with John, I'd shared a special bond with my dear Mr. Biscuits, and when I poured out my grief to him, it was almost like John's spirit was consoling my soul. Losing my four-legged little boy so soon after losing John was like a double whammy.

Michelle had adored Mr. Biscuits. She'd always had great compassion for any animal, but especially for dogs. I've already mentioned her own two dogs, which were as much her babies as Mr. Biscuits was my little boy.

"You can always rely on a dog," Michelle would often say, "but not always on a human being."

I finally decided I couldn't wait any longer to break the ice between us. As I've already mentioned, I knew Michelle had plans to travel down to Sydney sometime in December so she could spend a few days celebrating her Christmas birthday and the holiday season with family members who lived there. This was something she'd tried to do every year since she'd moved north to Queensland, especially now that her grandmother Gigi, whom she adored, was getting older and frailer.

My thought was to invite her over before she travelled so we could plan a birthday party for when she returned to the Gold Coast. Picking the perfect restaurant and menu would be something we could enjoy together as mother and daughter. Like all our family, Michelle loved fine food and dressing up. She was also an excellent cook herself, which wasn't surprising since her birth father was an outstanding chef and I too had a penchant for fine cuisine, so the art of cooking was in Michelle's very DNA.

Of course, my true hope was that we could talk out and lay to rest once and for all the issues that were keeping us apart. But with all the flurry of the elections and travelling down to cast our votes, I decided to put off the phone call until after the election results were in. The excitement of a Queenslander taking over as Prime Minister would be another positive topic of conversation that would bring us together.

But when I finally did call Michelle, as you already know, all I heard was that ridiculous cartoon character telling me to leave a message. And the next time the phone did ring in the early hours of Tuesday morning, November the 27th, it was a very different voice on the other end!

18

The Last Straw!

Any hope that Adam's confession was a false one, that my daughter might still emerge from some solitary retreat and come home to me, evaporated on Wednesday, December 5, 2007, as Adam led the police unhesitatingly to a heavily wooded section of Nerang Conservation Park not far off Belliss Road in Clagiraba, a Gold Coast community less than twenty kilometres from Michelle's home in Helensvale.

It was a beautiful area filled with state parks, bird and butterfly reserves, tall eucalyptus and gum forests, green-cloaked hills, frothing waterfalls, and crystal-clear creeks. Tourists flocked to the area to stroll along the scenic boardwalks or take a horseback or mountain bike excursion through the rain forest or up steep, green gullies into the hills. Black cockatoos could be seen and heard cracking open casuarina seeds from a tree branch perch overhead. Goannas or smaller lizards might be spotted sunbathing up a gum tree and even the occasional koala bear or spiny anteater.

Yes, it was a magnificent showpiece of God's creation. But on this Wednesday morning, it seemed fitting that the skies had opened up into a torrential rain, making it difficult for the police investigators and forensic team to slog through the wet brush and mud through which Adam claimed to have carried my daughter. That didn't keep them from quickly finding a shallow grave exactly where Adam had said it would be.

In it they found what was immediately identifiable as a young woman. The downpour was so heavy that it became a struggle for the forensic team to remove her body or preserve any semblance of the crime scene. It seemed as if heaven itself was weeping over the loss of a beautiful and beloved young life.

It had been 11:30 a.m. when the law enforcement team with Adam as their guide reached the grave site. As it was a forensic site a couple of days passed before the body could be transported from the scene. Only then did Detective Senior Sergeant P* call Stephen to bring him up to date on the new findings, so that my husband could in turn prepare me for what was about to unfold.

After the call, Stephen got immediately in touch with a close friend of mine, Di, who lived nearby. Explaining the developments he'd just learned from the detective, he asked if she would come over to keep an eye on me while he went down to the medical center to get a strong sedative from our doctor. He knew I would need it to help me cope with the news. Di was more than willing to help and soon arrived.

After Stephen returned with the medication, the three of us sat down to watch the 6.00 p.m. news. The familiar introductory sounds of the news program rang loud and clear. Then came the announcement: "Breaking News! Man confesses to the murder of his girlfriend Michelle Rigg, who has been missing for twelve days, and leads police to her grave site."

Reaching for Stephen and Di's hands, I squeezed them so hard I might have broken their bones if they hadn't stopped me. I stared at the TV set, not really taking in what was unfolding. I remember seeing Adam with his T-shirt over his face and flanked by two detectives as he was led to a police vehicle for transport to the Southport Watchhouse. Another news clip showed a forested area with police tape all around it and a forensic team searching for clues.

18 | The Last Straw!

I was too distraught to take in anything else the news anchor was saying. But in time, the details of this news report and many to follow became only too vivid in my mind. According to Adam's confession, his overriding motive was sheer, seething jealousy. He couldn't handle the thought of Michelle going out with someone else. In his twisted mind, if he couldn't have her, no one else would.

Detail by detail, the truth of that final evening of Michelle's life came out. She had returned around 5:30 p.m. from a long day at work, tired and in a bad mood. She'd caught up with email on her home computer, completed her normal daily exercise routine, then showered and prepared herself to go out with friends. This was the "date" with J* that had pushed Adam over the edge with jealous rage.

All the time, they had been quarrelling. Adam was still trying to talk Michelle into reconciling with him. He wanted her to stay home and have sex with him. She made bluntly clear that their relationship was over. She considered him no more than a flatmate to help pay the duplex's sizeable mortgage. And since he was behind in his rent by more than $2000AU, the least he could contribute was the occasional odd job he was doing around the duplex and helping care for the dogs.

As they bickered, Michelle continued drying and straightening her hair, painting her finger and toe nails, and dressing for her evening out. At some point, the quarrel intensified to the screaming match the neighbours had overheard. When she refused to break her "date" or have sex with him that evening, something snapped in Adam. Storming into the bedroom where she'd been getting dressed, he snatched the belt from Michelle's Telstra work uniform off a door knob where it was hanging.

In a fury, he then grabbed Michelle from behind and twisted the belt around her throat. As he did so, he pushed her face-down on the bed with his knee on her back. At 193.04 cm tall, he was about 30.5 cm taller than Michelle and close to twice her weight, so she didn't stand a chance. Her dogs were outside in the yard at the time, or they would have attacked him the moment he put his hands on her.

After her death, Adam realized that he couldn't leave Michelle to be discovered in the duplex. But he didn't have enough petrol in his car to drive far enough to dispose of her body where it wouldn't quickly be found. So he locked up the duplex, leaving the dogs corralled in the yard, and drove over to a nearby petrol station to fill up his fuel tank.

No one at the petrol station had noticed anything in Adam's demeanor to raise any red flags. Nor had the neighbours noticed anything when he returned to the duplex, loaded Michelle into the front seat, propped up as though she was sitting beside him, and drove away. That it was by now late at night and very dark out helped him get away with his monstrous actions.

For the next several hours, he drove around, looking for some unpopulated, isolated spot of bush where he could leave Michelle without her being discovered. At some point, he left the M1 interstate motorway that runs south from Helensvale, taking the exit onto Hwy 97, which leads west into the Clagiraba area with its many state and national forests. He then turned onto Clagiraba Road, a major thoroughfare that parallels the northern east-west boundary of Nerang Conservation Park.

At the far western end of the park, Clagiraba Creek forms a winding north-south border between the state forest and populated sections of Clagiraba. Just short of the creek, Adam took a right onto Belliss Road, which took him through the northwest entrance into Nerang Conservation Park. At this hour of the night, the park was empty of hikers and other holiday visitors or even park rangers. The forest canopy blocked out any light from moon and stars, so Adam would have had to bring along a light as well as digging tools.

Abandoning his car on the roadside, Adam carried his burden down a trail, then off into the scrub brush until a small stream blocked his progress. Satisfied no one would ever come across this isolated patch of bush, he dug a shallow grave, then left Michelle there without so much as bothering to cover her up. This wasn't just because he was in a hurry. In his confused mind, exposing her uncovered body to wildlife was a quick way of getting rid of the evidence.

Once he'd carried out his crime, he set off, as he'd originally told police, to visit friends for the rest of the weekend. Far from showing any indication of remorse, he'd spent the following hours gambling at a casino and hooking up with a prostitute. Sunday evening he'd come home to pretend he was only now discovering that Michelle had never returned home from her "walk".

Not all these details were included in that first 6 p.m. press briefing as the police laid out Adam's confession and the discoveries of the day. But it was more than enough that all I could do was sit there between Stephen and Di, staring at the TV set, stunned and speechless. It was such a strange feeling of despair and total hopelessness over which I had absolutely no control. Only a mother who has been there will understand what I'm talking about.

I can still remember Stephen and Di talking to me and holding me in an attempt to calm me down. Then suddenly the reality of what I was seeing on the TV screen hit me like salt poured into an open wound. I screamed so loudly it felt as though my throat was going to tear open. I must have sounded like a wounded animal.

The pain in my throat was excruciating, and I couldn't breathe. All I could think of was that my precious daughter was dead and this sick, inhuman monster had stolen her from me. He'd taken her life for no reason. WHY? He was supposed to love her. Now because of his selfishness, I would never see her pretty face nor hear her voice again. I wanted to shake him until he fell to the ground gasping for air just as she had, then lie there lifeless.

"No, no, I can't bear it!" I screamed out. "I don't want to live anymore!"

Di, bless her heart, stayed with me until after I had taken the sedative Stephen had brought home, followed by a couple of stiff whiskies. What happened the rest of that night, I couldn't recall. I finally went to bed, crying myself into some sort of numbness, though I wouldn't call it sleep because I could still hear myself muttering, "No, it can't be! Tell me it's not true. It wasn't Michelle after all, was it? She's not dead. Not my Michelle! The police must have made a mistake. It does happen, you know! I'm sure it's not her. She'll come home in the morning, you'll see."

But of course, she never did.

19

Wounded to the Core

For the following week or so, the forensic team was all over Michelle's home. Even though Adam had confessed to her murder, they still had to find corroborating physical evidence. The police turned the duplex upside down, looking for the murder weapon—the belt to Michelle's Telstra uniform—and anything else that would prove indisputably that the crime had taken place in her home and that Adam had been the perpetrator.

Adam himself claimed in his confession to have thrown the belt as well as Michelle's handbag into the duplex's wheelie bin. The scheduled garbage pickup for that neighbourhood was Monday morning. Which might be another reason he'd delayed reporting her missing until Monday evening, since that week's garbage would by then be buried in mountains of rubbish and virtually impossible to retrieve.

Since neither belt nor handbag were ever found, we never found out if Adam was telling the truth on this point. This might seem a minor detail. But it turned out to be extremely significant to the prosecution of the case and frustrating to me. The autopsy made clear that Adam had been at least partially successful in hiding his crime as weather, decomposition, and animal activity had made it impossible to determine with any certainty the cause of death.

Without an actual murder weapon, even a confession might not be enough to ensure the conviction of murder and lifetime sentence Adam's crime deserved. In fact, with no physical proof that he was the perpetrator, by the time his case ever came to trial he could be out with little more than time already served. Which might be exactly the kind of wild goose chase Adam had in mind in sending the police to search through mountains of rotting garbage for the contents of that wheelie-bin.

In truth, he could have dumped them in some remote gully as impossible to locate without a guide as Michelle's grave had been. After all, why would he keep such incriminating evidence in his own garbage bin for three full days? Maybe those muddy shoes the police had found in the garbage bin *after* Adam claimed the garbage company had collected her belt and handbag were from such a trek.

But then, why didn't he dispose of her mobile phone too? Or was he worried all that high-tech law enforcement had these days could track its GPS signal into the wilderness? Who knew what was going on in that twisted, confused mind? In the end, whether Adam was lying or not, the strategy did work since without corroborating physical evidence (somehow, Adam guiding the police to her grave wasn't enough!), the case dragged on and on.

I cannot put into words just how all this made me feel. According to the tenets of grief counseling, it is a completely natural process for anger to follow grief. This certainly made sense to me because I discovered that I was very angry. Not just angry, but in a fuming, livid, furious, teeth-gnashing rage!

One overwhelming reason for my fury was that I couldn't understand why this whole nightmare had happened to me. Why had my only child been taken from me in such a brutal manner? Especially when she had so much to live for. It stands to reason that children shouldn't depart this world before their parents, right?

I would have given my life to save hers! It should have been me, not her! I

19 | Wounded to the Core

screamed at myself. Or maybe I was screaming at God. In all honesty, trading places with Michelle would have suited me to a T, given the grief and pain I had experienced losing a beloved brother, a four-legged "son", and now my only daughter within six months. I had still been trying to come to terms with the first two when this new tragedy took place, and the awful devastation of it hit me like a ton of bricks.

At that moment, I felt one hundred percent qualified to suggest that no one else on this earth could possibly feel the way I did. Not unless they had been subjected to the same scenario, under the same circumstances as I had. My head was spinning so that I felt all over the place. In fact, I truly thought I was going mad. I didn't know how to handle this kind of grief. How could I? All I really wanted was to be with my child, and if that meant being with her in heaven instead of on earth, so be it!

What made my grief and anger more difficult to deal with were the well-intended friends and family members who would say things like, "I know it hurts right now, but it will get better in time. Time heals all wounds."

Or, "Don't be sad! Don't cry! She wouldn't want you to."

Or, "She's happy now. She's not hurting anymore. You'll see her again in heaven, so rejoice!"

I didn't want to seem ungrateful, and I understood that they meant well. But at that particular moment, I certainly didn't feel like rejoicing. The worst was when they would say, "I know how you feel!" This happened over and over, and since they really had no idea how I felt, I thought it was totally inappropriate.

What would they know? I fumed silently. The only way for these well-wishers to get a glimpse of what I was going through was to experience for themselves the absolute nightmare I was living.

I love the song lyrics by Michael Bolton: "You say it best when you say nothing at all." There's a lot of truth in those lyrics as silence can indeed be golden on occasion, and when you are engaging in conversation with a grieving person, it is important to take time to analyze the situation before speaking—or simply say nothing at all!

One small comfort in this time period came through my husband Stephen. When Detective Senior Sergeant P* had first called with the bad news, Stephen had wanted to visit Michelle's makeshift grave. His reason for going was to put his mind at ease and get some confirmation that the site matched the vision we'd both received from God earlier.

At the time, the detective inspector declined his request since the grave site was still an active crime scene and no one was allowed near it. But some days later when the forensic team was finished with the site, he did manage to get permission. Turning onto Belliss Road, Stephen drove all the way to the end where a boom gate prevented vehicle access into the actual state forest. Parking the car on the shoulder of the road, Stephen walked past the long bar that extended across the road, then continued on foot down a pebble track.

About twenty-five metres down the path, he came across the first of a line of bright-orange tags. These had been tacked onto tree branches about the height of a man's head by the police escort on duty when Adam guided them to Michelle's body. Stephen followed the tags straight to where that sick monster had dumped my precious daughter like an unwanted load.

Once Stephen reached the site, he was able to confirm that it was indeed a remote forest area with tall trees like the vision God had given us. There was also a brook less than a metre from Michelle's makeshift grave. This, along with Wednesday's heavy rain, left the ground underfoot marshy and damp, just like the revelation God had given me personally. To Stephen, in the midst of all the uncertainty swirling around us, having clear evidence that God had answered our plea for Michelle's location was very comforting.

And to me as well when he shared it with me. It was a comfort I desperately needed right then. As reality continued to sink in, I felt unbearably miserable, and I wanted God to do something about it.

"God, please help me!" I cried out.

There was no response. Why wasn't there a 1-800-4-HEAVEN number people could call when they desperately needed answers from God the way there were 1-800 numbers for so many less urgent issues? Okay, maybe there was one called prayer. I knew I had important questions I needed answered then and there, so I cried out again heavenward, "Hello, is somebody there?"

Still no answer. I went on, "God, I'm fuming! I'm so angry I think I could kill that so-and-so. But I know I can't do that, so I'm asking you to do something. Can't you make him pay for his crime?"

At that very moment, I felt something supernatural taking hold of me and I heard myself crying out, "Lord, I pray that this miserable sod sees my Michelle's face when he wakes up in the morning until he goes to sleep at night every day for the rest of his life as a reminder of his cowardly and brutal act. In Jesus's precious name, I pray this. Amen."

My mother always said that God hears a mother's cry and feels her pain, especially at times like these when grief is too much to bear. This I can now testify to be true.

20

An Unbearable Task

God brought another and even more significant comfort into my life during this period, and this one too came through my husband Stephen. As with the grave site, Michelle's home had remained an active crime scene. But as her closest family members, Stephen and I were invited to go through the duplex and take home any of her belongings we wanted to keep.

"Just take your time," one kindly female Police Officer told me. "You never know what precious keepsakes you might find."

I was touched and amazed when the officer took it upon herself to lead the way through the duplex, picking up various items to bring them to my attention as though she was well aware I had no idea where to start. She had clearly been down that same road with previous homicide victims.

It was just a few days later when, like the forest grave site, the police announced they had finished their investigation of the duplex. This meant it was no longer an active crime scene, so once the forensic team left, it was turned over to the family—i.e., me as Michelle's mum. Stephen and I had already decided to put the residence up for sale as quickly as possible. Now we would need to empty the duplex of its entire contents, sort out what we wanted to keep, dispose of what

20 | An Unbearable Task

we didn't want, then get the cleaners in so that the house would look presentable for a real estate agent to take over.

Of course, I wanted to keep every single object of clothing, photographs, you name it, that belonged to my daughter. In reality, I couldn't as many items had been damaged by the various chemicals the forensic team used to test for DNA, gather fingerprints, and other evidence. And we didn't have space in our own home to store all Michelle's possessions, so I had to be very selective.

Even so, I grabbed everything I could because I desperately needed to hang on to something, anything, belonging to my beautiful daughter that would help me feel close to her. Her clothing still carried the sweet fragrance that was a mixture of her shampoo, perfume, hand soap, and other scents. I would bury my nose in them, as though smelling them could bring her close again. I longed to feel her continued presence around me, even if just through her material possessions.

Just give me anything of hers to hold and smell, or I'll go mad! I cried out silently. But as keen as I was to go through it all with a fine-tooth comb, I found that I couldn't do it. The police search had trashed the beautiful home of which my daughter had been so proud, and to even think of sifting through that mess made me sick.

I went out into the garden where Michelle and I had shared such a beautiful moment when she was showing off her new home to me. But even there the yard she'd cared for so meticulously was now a mess of torn-up sod and holes the police had dug in their search. Sitting in the same seat where we had sat together, I burst into uncontrollable sobs. The situation eventually became unbearable for me to the point that I couldn't stay any longer. Gathering a few precious keepsakes, I left to Stephen the task of salvaging what he could on my behalf.

I had returned home when Stephen called me. In his search through the piled-up rubble left by the forensics team, he had come across the Bible he had once given Michelle. She had kept it after all, and a glance through its pages made clear she had read it. To me, this alone was a miracle, as I had hoped and prayed throughout her troubled, dark years in the drug scene that she would seek refuge in God's Word.

For the first time since Michelle's brutal murder, I found some small cause for rejoicing.

This wasn't a "Praise God!" cheery type of rejoicing because I was still filled with painful grief. It was more an inward comforting of my very soul like no other feeling I've known. I had no doubt it was the Holy Spirit. Jesus himself, when he was comforting his disciples over his impending death (John 14-16), assured them that he would send to them a *parakletos* (John 14:16-17, 26; 15:26; 16:7), the Holy Spirit of God who would indwell them in his place.

According to which Bible version you read, the original Greek word *parakletos* is translated as comforter, counselor, helper, or even advocate. But the word literally means someone who comes alongside to offer support and help in time of need. This was what I felt from the Holy Spirit at that moment and in the long months and years ahead.

But Stephen went on to share more good news. Inside the Bible he'd found a gospel tract. The tract had a section for the reader to write down their own response, and in that section in Michelle's own handwriting was recorded her acceptance of Jesus as her personal Lord and Saviour. Wow! This was definitively the power of prayer in all its glory. How many times had we beseeched God over and over to reach deep into my precious daughter's heart and draw her to himself?

And at the eleventh hour, he'd done just that. From Michelle's scribbled handwriting, it seemed that in her personal turmoil when things were going so rough for her, she'd turned to that Bible for answers and made her pledge to surrender her life to Jesus, much as I had done so many years ago in my own turmoil.

At that painful time, this was just the good news I needed to hear. I felt an enormous relief as if God's loving hand had lifted from my chest a heavy weight that had been suffocating me since the murder. In its place a much-needed feeling of peace filled my heart to overflowing. *Thank you, Jesus! My precious little princess has been redeemed.*

Shortly after Michelle's body was found, we received an email from a very good friend of ours, Pastor S*. He was flying back from the United States to Australia at the time, but was very much aware of what was going on since Stephen had been sharing updates and requests for prayer with his email contacts. Pastor S* was waiting for a flight at Los Angeles International Airport (LAX) in California when he sent us an email to share that he had received a revelation from God that Michelle was safe with him in heaven. Stephen immediately responded, sharing about the Bible and Michelle's hand-written note that he'd found.

"That's great news!" Pastor S* responded, then added that we should expect another two revelations to confirm Michelle's salvation and presence with God in heaven.

Now you, my reader, may think this sounds crazy (and that's entirely your prerogative), but just hold on while I give some explanation as to why the pastor would have said this. The number three has great significance in Scripture. The Israelites were commanded to appear before God three times each year. God called the prophet Samuel three times in the night when he was a child. Elijah poured water three times over the altar before God sent down fire from heaven.

In the New Testament, Jesus prayed three times in Gethsemane. Jesus was crucified at the third hour and raised on the third day. After Peter denied Jesus three times, Jesus asked three times if Peter loved him. And later Peter himself received a vision from God that was repeated three times. The apostle Paul asked God three times to take away his "thorn in the flesh", and three times God said no. And so on.

According to biblical scholars, the number three is used by God to get our attention, to emphasize the importance of an event, or show completeness. If you are interested, you can find many studies on this topic online. It is also the number of God himself—Father, Son, and

Holy Spirit, the Godhead Three-in-One, or the Trinity. In 1 John 5:7, we are told: "For there are three that bear witness in heaven, the Father, the Word, and the Holy Spirit, and these three are one."

So it is not so crazy after all that God would reveal to our pastor friend that he would be sending three revelations concerning Michelle. At the time, Stephen and I didn't think much about it. We already had faith that Michelle was in heaven, since when any individual is willing to give their life to Jesus and accept him as Lord and Saviour, their sins are forgiven and they are guaranteed a place in Heaven to spend eternity with him.

Nevertheless, as further events transpired, we couldn't help but connect them with the words God had laid on the heart of Pastor S* to share with us. Events that would bring us even more comfort and cause for rejoicing.

21

Ineffable Times

The coroner had also finally released Michelle's body for burial. The next step was to transport her by hearse to Sydney, where she would finally be laid to rest. I chose Sydney because that was her birthplace and where she had been the happiest in her all-too-short life. She often said to me, "You know Mum, we should have never left Sydney because we were so happy there."

Yes, we were, my darling, I assured her mentally, *and now you're going back.*

In truth, I was still so angry with the Gold Coast and entire territory of Queensland at this juncture that I wanted to run away and forget I had ever set foot there because to me it felt that this place had stolen my precious little girl. Leaving even for that short period to make arrangements in Sydney and plan the funeral was such a relief. If possible, I would have shaken the dust of the Gold Coast off my shoes forever!

Michelle's funeral was scheduled exactly one week after what would have been her twenty-ninth birthday. I had chosen a cremation instead of a burial. As I looked at the calendar, I realized that she was murdered two weeks before her birthday and cremated one week after. What a big role this important date, her birthday, had played in her death as well as her life.

I wondered if maybe it had happened like this so that I would never forget. But then, how could I? Those dates were like flashing neon lights in my head. And in truth, every year since those dates have triggered my emotions in a way impossible to describe. Her birth and death will be forever inscribed in my heart, never to be erased until the day I die.

Numbness had set in by the time I arrived in Sydney. I had been through this before with John's death as well as my father's, so my robot mode kicked in, taking everything in stride as though I was in Sydney for somebody else's funeral, not Michelle's. What made things worse was that the funeral directors wouldn't allow me to see her.

Of course, the reality was that after all she'd been exposed to, her body would not have been a sight for the faint-hearted, let alone the mother of the victim. But at that crucial moment, I didn't really care. I just wanted to see my little girl's face. To touch her and whisper sweet nothings in her ear. If nothing else, it would give this wounded mother some closure. But though I begged them to let me say goodbye to my little girl for the last time, they were adamant in refusing, much to my sorrow.

Still, at least I was able to choose a perfect outfit for my daughter's final journey. In Australia, as in many countries, it is customary to provide a final outfit for the deceased in case the family opts for a viewing or wake before cremation or burial. In our case the viewing wasn't allowed, but the clothing would still be provided as a mark of respect for the deceased and immediate family.

I went right through Michelle's clothing, trying to pick something that would appropriately reflect the person she had been—my princess. I chose a white outfit, but the top was too plain for my Michelle, so I decided to add a special touch of love by sewing in pearls to embellish it and add a "princess" touch. By the time I finished with it, I knew my baby would look so pretty that she would turn heads even in heaven.

21 | Ineffable Times

All in white, she would most probably be the cutest angel in God's Kingdom.

Jack offered to go with me to deliver the outfit to the funeral home as well as to choose a coffin. He still regarded Michelle as his daughter and had kept in touch with her until the end. He had been devastated by her death and had immediately volunteered to assist me with all the funeral preparations in Sydney, where he still lived. It was one last thing he could do for his little girl.

Stephen wanted to be by my side at the funeral as well. But he was dealing with other important matters concerning her death for me on the Gold Coast. This included having her beloved doggies put down. Having witnessed the murder of their "mummy", they were too traumatized to be placed in a new home. It was the kindest choice under the circumstances, but a hard call for Stephen to deal with in my absence. He also finished clearing out Michelle's house, which I couldn't have faced doing, so I was very grateful for that.

Jack and I had finalized the funeral arrangements, after which he kindly drove me back to Mum's place, where I was staying. Just as I walked up to the front door, Mum came running out to tell me that her pastor was on the phone, but she couldn't quite understand what he wanted. In all her years in Australia, Mum had never fully mastered the English language, so she still needed an interpreter to understand the pastor and other church members, especially for phone conversations. And her children were always happy to translate for her.

Running to the phone, I picked it up. "Hello, Pastor H*. What can I do for you? Are you wanting to speak with Gloria?"

Gloria attended the same church and was Mum's usual contact person for the church staff. But Pastor H* immediately responded, "No, no, it's you I wanted to speak to."

I was caught off-guard since while I too had attended that church when I first became a Christian in 1994, I didn't really know this particular pastor. Cautiously, I asked, "Oh, why is that?"

"Well, this morning I had a vision from God," Pastor H* responded. "I saw your brother John and your daughter with Jesus in heaven. So I just had to call you. I wanted to let you know not to worry about whether your daughter is saved. She did indeed accept Jesus as her Saviour and is redeemed for all eternity in heaven."

I was stunned at his words. I managed to gather my wits to respond, "Thank you so much, Pastor H*. That is actually is very meaningful to me right now!"

Wow! Without any prompting on our part, a pattern was taking place here. Interesting, very interesting! This had to be the second revelation of which Pastor S* had spoken. As I hung up the phone, I was already praying that we would receive the third one as Pastor S* had mentioned.

22

Goodbye, my Angel

We gathered to say farewell to our Michelle, family and friends alike, in a small church in Paddington, New South Wales, not far from the hospital where she was born. I had decided to carry out her funeral in a different manner than the usual. My precious daughter was still single and had never enjoyed the beautiful wedding of her dreams. So as with the bridal-white outfit I'd chosen, I wanted to make her funeral representative of a wedding.

It was the least I could do for my baby girl, and I only had one shot at it. To begin with, I organized the reverse of a traditional funeral service where the coffin is placed at the front of the church, then family and friends are invited in to pay their respects. I had family and friends seated first as would be done at a wedding venue. Then Michelle entered the church all in white and beautiful flowers as a bride would be when she walked down the aisle to her groom.

I had chosen a white casket with white roses that had just a tinge of pink above the handles and frangipanis on top. The pallbearers were dressed in white as well. Their outfits were topped with exquisite burgundy wide-brimmed hats, and together they offered a striking, elegant touch to the procession.

I had also arranged to adorn the entire church with beautiful flowers. I had chosen a magnificent giant heart made up of roses and tulips to display next to her photo. As she was wheeled down the aisle, it felt as though she was advancing joyously to meet her heavenly bridegroom at the altar, Jesus, her Lord and Saviour, with whom she would spend eternity as part of the bride of Christ (Ephesians 5:25-27; Revelation 19:7-9; 21:2).

I cried, oh, how I cried! But as devastating and sad as this scene was, it was also breathtaking and even magical to me, and I felt overwhelmed with pride in my daughter as well as grief. It is an unforgettable memory I will never get tired of revisiting, despite the inevitable lump in my throat and tears it brings to my eyes. Goodbye, my darling girl, until we meet again in eternity!

For the life of me, I have no idea how I managed to get through that day, the toughest of my life. What a horrible moment for any parent to endure! How could anyone get over that? I was truly amazed at my own composure. It was then I that recognized that God was carrying me in his own loving arms, as I didn't have the strength to walk on my own.

The funeral was on a Saturday. The next morning, my siblings Tony and Gloria were planning as usual to attend their local church and asked me to come along. Close to ninety years old by now, Mum no longer left the house on Sunday mornings, but she insisted I attend church with my brother and sister. I didn't want to go anywhere. My thoughts were still at the funeral, and all I could visualize was Michelle's white coffin covered with frangipanis coming towards me. I felt numb, a feeling that was becoming very familiar.

Tony understood my feelings and backed away from pushing me to come. But Mum kept insisting as only she could, and I finally gave in and went to church with my two siblings. Having attended the funeral, Pastor H* and his wife were very aware of our grief and sympathetic towards us. They shared with the congregation the circumstances of Michelle's demise. Then they asked everyone there to join them in

22 | Goodbye, my Angel

prayer, specifically for God to help me deal with my own personal grief, having just lost my only child as victim of a homicide.

As they prayed, tears poured down my face, followed by uncontrollable sobs. I was totally inconsolable. All I remember of the rest of that service was being held and comforted by the pastor's wife. After the service, it was customary to linger for fellowship over a cup of coffee or tea, chatting with friends or welcoming visitors. Tony and Gloria mingled with their friends, but were very much aware that I was in no condition to hang around for long. The fact was, I just wanted to go home. Gathering my things, I went to find my siblings and ask for them to take me home.

Just then, I was approached out of nowhere by a lady who immediately started talking to me. She asked, "Are you the mother of the girl who was murdered?"

As I nodded, she proceeded to tell me that she had arrived from England just the day before. She was staying in a hotel and had asked for information on a church to attend that Sunday. Someone at the hotel who knew this church had suggested she try the morning service here, which she'd done.

"Obviously, I don't know anyone here," she went on, "but when the pastor mentioned your daughter, I received a vision from God. It was of a young lady with long, dark-brown hair wearing a crown of flowers on her head. She was smiling and looked happy."

"That's lovely," I responded. "But what does it have to do with my daughter, and what does the crown of flowers signify?"

She gave me a kind smile. "Well, in the olden days in England, it was customary for young brides to wear a crown of flowers as a headdress on their wedding day. Does that have any significance to you?"

Did it ever! I was absolutely blown away by what I had just heard coming out of the mouth of a total stranger. She had never met me before and could have had no knowledge of how I had arranged Michelle's funeral to be representative of a wedding. Not just a wedding, but of my sweet daughter going to meet her heavenly Bridegroom, Jesus Christ, dressed as a bride with flowers in her hair.

I was so grateful that Mum insisted I attend that Sunday service, difficult as it was for me. If I hadn't, I would have missed out on revelation number three! For me, this woman's words were confirmation of the prophetic word God had given to Pastor S*. It wasn't that three revelations were necessary to ensure Michelle's salvation. As I've said before, from the moment Michelle accepted Jesus as her Lord and Saviour, her sins were forgiven and she was granted salvation, redemption, and eternal life in heaven.

It was more that God knew I needed reassurance that my daughter had placed her faith in Jesus before it was too late. And indeed, with all that had happened, all that I'd gone through in recent years with Michelle, her rebellion and other problems, I did need that absolute assurance as otherwise enduring her murder, loss, and cremation would all be too much to bear. My loving heavenly Father had reached down to speak through three very different sources, one a complete stranger to me, just to let this hurting mother's heart know that my precious child was now safe and happy in heaven with her heavenly Father and Bridegroom.

I must confess there was a kind of happiness in my heart at this time, even though it was laced with sadness. On the one hand, I was over the moon to have had such unmistakable confirmation from God of Michelle's salvation. On the other, I was left with a broken heart in realizing that she was gone and that I would never see her again.

At least in this lifetime.

23

My New Normal

I remained in Sydney until Michelle's ashes were released, along with the paperwork necessary to bring her home to Queensland by plane. When I checked in at the airport, I showed the airline representative behind the counter the authorization letter from the funeral home. I could see sadness in her eyes as well as awkwardness over what to say to me. All I could do was look right back at her, trying my utmost not to burst into tears. I knew I had to take control of my emotions lest they trigger a panic attack, and I certainly didn't want that in mid-air.

Thank goodness, I was still in "robot mode" so I managed to get through security gates without a major meltdown. I was carrying the package that contained Michelle's ashes in a bag as hand luggage. The package itself looked just like a shoe box, and except for a label with my daughter's name on it, no one would have been the wiser.

I myself had trouble believing it really was my daughter in that box. Since I hadn't had the closure of actually seeing Michelle before her cremation, part of me persisted in believing she was still alive and going about her own life on the Gold Coast. The other part wondered what was really in that box. Then I would remind myself, *Hang on a minute! This is your daughter you're holding. You've got to be careful with it!*

My internal conversation continued as I boarded the plane. *Are you insane? What are you doing, woman, carrying on like a lunatic and crying at a drop of a hat? Stop! No one knows what's in that bag. People are going to think you're strange cradling it like that! Anyway, how can you just carry your daughter's ashes onto a plane as if there was just a pair of shoes in that box? What's wrong with you? Get real or go see a shrink!*

Then my "robot mode" would creep back in, and I would become a cool, calm, and collected person catching a flight back home with a very precious cargo in hand. But panic would once again raise its ugly head, and I would ask myself, *Have you completely lost your mind? What are you going to do with her ashes on the plane? Where do you intend to put them? Why didn't you leave them in Sydney where they belonged?*

My brain was almost exploding with the conflicting conversations taking place in it at any given moment. I wanted to shout out, "Leave me alone! I don't know why I brought them with me. I just know I can't bear to be away from my daughter one minute longer. We've been apart far too long. I've just got to have her close to me right now. Is that a crime? Go away, voices!"

Somehow, I made it through the flight. When the plane touched down at the Gold Coast airport, Stephen was waiting to drive me and my precious parcel home. Once in the car, he mentioned in a nonchalant way that he had a surprise waiting for me back at the house.

"I hope it's not another bird. I don't want another bird!" I responded immediately. After my brother John's death and the loss of our Mr. Biscuits, Stephen had bought me a canary, whom we named Sunny Boy, in the hope that having another living creature to love and care for would help me deal with my grief.

One reason for his choice was because I had adamantly refused to replace Mr. Biscuits with another puppy. I was tired of getting emotionally attached and then facing the inevitable pain of loss when a pet died. In my mind, Stephen and I were on the same page about not getting another dog. So it was a shock when we walked into the house, and there at the top of the stairs just where Mr. Biscuits used to stand

23 | My New Normal

was Stephen's surprise—a beautiful collie that looked just like Lassie from the TV shows.

Stephen had decided to look for a dog while I was away in Sydney for Michelle's funeral, still convinced this would help me with the healing process. Since I'd refused to get another puppy, he'd thought that a full-grown dog already housebroken and in need of less constant care would be able to offer me immediate comfort and support. Since Mr. Biscuits had been a collie, he'd gone on line and googled collie breeders in South East Queensland.

He'd found a four-year-old male purebred "rough" collie used for breeding purposes until his owner discovered that the dog was vision-impaired. The breeder had immediately abandoned the dog once he was no longer useful for breeding. A lady had rescued him and was now looking for the right person to give him a good home.

Stephen was touched by the dog's sad story, but he also felt led by the Holy Spirit that this was just the right new member God had chosen for our family. So two days earlier, he had driven over to bring the dog home. Only to be faced with a very angry new mistress. I must admit I reacted poorly because of where I was at emotionally.

"No way! You promised me you wouldn't get another dog!" I shouted at Stephen. "I don't want him. You can just take him back to where you got him."

Looking back, I am ashamed at the way I behaved toward this poor innocent creature. He just wanted to love me and share my pain. But the surprise was too overwhelming, and my heart had been broken into too many pieces to be able to express love at that moment, even to a gorgeous collie. Only God could mend my broken heart, but that would take time. A long time.

So when I saw him waiting at the top of the stairs, wagging his tail, undernourished, shy, and afraid of failing the first test of acceptance, I panicked. Completely ignoring the dog, I pushed past to carry my precious package into my study. Trembling with his tail between his legs, the collie went straight back to Stephen, with whom he had already formed a bond over the last two days.

Stephen stooped down to comfort him. "Don't worry, boy! She'll come around, you'll see. Just give her some time."

My husband was smart enough to ignore my bad attitude because he knew that sooner or later my heart would relent. And indeed, Stephen was right. Our new family member began to grow on me, and I came to realize very quickly that this really had been a "God-idea" on Stephen's part. I found myself talking to him more and more, recounting stories about Mr. Biscuits, who was a purebred "Lassie" dog just like him. We named him Prince after the "Prince of Peace" (Isaiah 9:6), because that's what he brought to our home—peace, much needed peace.

So there we were—Stephen and me, Sunny Boy, and Prince. But no Michelle, just her ashes. I had already decided the "shoe box" was too simple and banal for my little girl's final resting place. So as soon as I could, I bought a beautiful little treasure chest adorned with golden leaves and placed her ashes inside. I knew my princess would approve of my choice as we had similar taste in most things. It felt right and comforting to have her close to me in that magnificent treasure chest because she was indeed my one and only treasure.

At that moment, I realized this was the beginning of my "new normal" because life as I had known it was never going to be the same again. The person I was had died the day Michelle was murdered, and I had to give this "new normal" a go because if I ignored it, I wouldn't be able to climb out of the dark pit in which I was slowly being engulfed. I had to be strong, stronger than I had ever been before, so much stronger. I also had to accept that never in my lifetime was I going to see my daughter again.

That was when I recognized I just could not do this alone. At that very moment, I turned to God and cried out, *Help me!*

And God did. Right then and there, I could feel a supernatural

23 | My New Normal

Presence all around me, reassuring me that I wasn't alone. In my inner spirit, I could sense God's Holy Spirit encouraging me, *It's going to be a tough road ahead, but you're going to get through it, you'll see! I know it's difficult for you to get your head around it right now because you're hurting, but trust me, I know!*

That sweet assurance was a tremendous comfort to me, just as Scripture promises (2 Corinthians 1:3-4). The future might not look bright at the moment, but there was a promise of a "silver lining" somewhere ahead.

24

Extending Forgiveness

My own little "Prince of Peace" was definitely part of that silver lining as the months passed. For some reason we began calling him "Puppy", and the name stuck. I guess because he had such a youthful appearance and always wanted to play. Mind you, he was a great dancer too. He loved music. Any time I switched on the Sound System and started to dance on my own, he would join me, jumping up to my level and resting his front paws on my shoulders.

Altogether, he was "just what the doctor ordered", as they say, at this critical time in my life. I needed to talk to someone who wouldn't answer back and who would love me unconditionally. Puppy fitted that description perfectly.

Which was a blessing I desperately needed because I was still very angry and couldn't bring myself to care much about anything or anyone—including my husband. Our first Christmas and New Year without Michelle went by in a blur, and I couldn't stop crying. As one month passed, then two, then three, I still felt so lost. I knew that I looked a mess, a mere shadow of the successful, composed business woman I had once been. But it didn't matter to me at that point in time. I had bigger things on my mind like trying to deal with the invasion in my house.

By this I mean Michelle's things, which were everywhere. There wasn't a moment in the day or a place in our home that I didn't have to "face" her. I knew this situation couldn't go on, but neither could I bear the thought of parting with her things. Now and then I would go through her belongings, packing, unpacking, and then repacking them, weeping despairingly over every single piece of clothing.

Along with my grief, I was also battling a continued sense of guilt and blame. If only I had been more attentive to my daughter's feelings, she'd still be alive. If only I had called her instead of holding off, we would have made up and she'd still be around. It was all my fault. No, it was Stephen's fault for not having a better relationship with her! No, I didn't know anymore and didn't care *whose* fault it was. The fact was that with the snap of a finger she'd disappeared out of my life never to be seen again.

In time I came to the realization that, despite all my "if onlys", there was nothing in my power I could have done to prevent this tragedy. It was never my call to make, not in a million years. Michelle's life and death were in God's hands, and it was just her appointed hour.

But all my anger and loss of interest in everything and everyone inevitably impacted my relationship with Stephen. We weren't the first one to experience such a problem. Studies on couples who have been victims of a homicide show that seventy to eighty percent of those couples end up divorced. The way things were evolving, I could see that Stephen and I were heading that way fast.

Our pastor at the time suggested grief counselling, so I gave it a try. But I wasn't ready to listen nor willing to be guided into some sort of "step by step" routine. The counselor would say something like, "It's not your fault, you know."

"Hello, I know it's not my fault!" I would respond. "And I think you're wasting my time and yours. Let's move on!"

I eventually called it quits. All I could do now was turn to God in despair and shout, "Please help me!"

When I could feel no immediate heavenly response, I would turn to Prince, giving him a big hug, and all my worries would momentarily dissipate much as they do for a child who runs crying to their mother to have some small hurt blown away with a kiss and a hug. Prince had the most amazing, knowing eyes, and when I gazed into them, I would immediately feel peace, comfort, and most importantly, love. God's love reaching out to me through this gift of his as though to say, "Don't worry, my child. Everything's going to be all right, you'll see!"

Unfortunately, those feelings never lasted long. Reality would creep in, and I would fall back into the dark pit with no idea of how to avoid it. Or maybe I didn't have the urge anymore because it was way too comfortable down there. Safe even in a weird way. Being in that pit gave me the excuse not to do anything I didn't want to do. After all, as a grieving mother, how could it be expected of me?

There was only one thing wrong with that theory. I had Jesus in me, which meant I could tap into the heavenly realm and call on God's Holy Spirit at any time to get the strength I needed to carry on. And I had always been a fighter. What kind of a quitter was I to be giving up this easily?

For the first time in my life, I had reached rock bottom, and it was scary, very scary. I was in such a somber place I could see no sign of light anywhere I looked. Lost and in despair, I knew only one way out of this nightmare, and that was to pass all my worries over to my heavenly Father. Which meant I needed to have a chat with him right now!

I looked up towards heaven. I was so angry that I shouted out, "God, what am I meant to do? Adam killed my daughter. I don't have any other children. I'm at my wits end! So what are you going to do about it? How on earth did you let this happen? You're supposed to protect children from evil. Why didn't you protect her? You could have stopped Adam if you had wanted to, but you didn't. Why?"

Almost on cue, I heard in my mind a calming, soothing response. *It was her time, just like it was John's. Accept it and leave it all to me.*

"What do you mean, accept it?" I shouted back. "What about justice? Are we ever going to see justice come out of this mess? Who is going to punish him?"

Hush, child, hush! I heard, then silence.

Even though I believed God had answered me, I had a hard time coming to grips with that answer. Michelle was dead, gone forever, while Adam was still alive and we, the taxpayers, were making sure he had all the comforts jail could provide. Was that fair? In my opinion, the law was far too lenient when it came to domestic violence.

I told God exactly how I felt. When I finally stopped, once again that same calming voice broke the silence. *I know you are angry, child. But let vengeance be mine. All I want you to do is to forgive him. Leave the rest to me.*

I knew what God was saying to me as I'd read similar passages in Scripture. From the very beginning when God had given the Israelites his law, he had told them to leave vengeance to him. In the New Testament, that same command had been reiterated:

Do not seek revenge my friends, but leave room for God's wrath, for it is written: "It is mine to avenge; I will repay," says the Lord. (Romans 12:19; see also Deuteronomy 32:35)

Still, I couldn't believe what I was hearing. "What do you mean, forgive him? I can't do that! He killed my daughter!"

Just do it! God's answer was firm and final. I knew I had to be obedient, and in that instant my way of thinking changed dramatically.

Who am I to hate this person? I suddenly realized. *If Jesus can forgive our sins and willingly offer his life for us on the cross to give us eternal life, how can I profess to be a Christian and not forgive my daughter's murderer?*

It became very clear to me that what God was asking me to do was a mere drop in the ocean compared to what he in Jesus Christ had endured on the cross to pay for our sins. And I needed to do it quickly and willingly. After all, I'd never professed to be a saint. If I needed forgiveness of my sins, so did Adam.

I also knew that remaining resentful and unforgiving would not bring Michelle back. On the contrary, it would only make me a bitter, twisted old woman, and I knew my daughter wouldn't want that for me! Unforgiveness is like a cancer. Unless you get a hold of it in the early stages and claim victory, it will keep raising its ugly head again, leading to all kinds of sickness and other negative conditions. At the end of the day, only by forgiving your adversary will you find genuine peace in your heart.

There and then, I truly forgave Adam for murdering my daughter. I felt no more hatred towards him, only pity for his personal weakness and lack of control. I had fulfilled my commitment and obeyed my heavenly Father, leaving me with a clear conscience.

Having said that, I still felt that justice had to be done. In my opinion, Adam still had to pay for his crime. He should receive some sort of punishment for his brutal act. But just what that meant wasn't up to me. God had asked me to forgive my daughter's murderer and leave the rest to him.

And that is what I did.

25

A 'Country' Change

But though I had committed to forgiving Adam, I was still battling with depression and grief. Remaining in the same place where I had lost my daughter became increasingly unbearable because her presence was everywhere. I could see her on every street corner and in every shopping mall. I even heard her coming up the front steps of our house.

If that wasn't torment enough, I would burst into tears every time I saw a little girl hand-in-hand with her mummy. I was weeping constantly. I couldn't even drive anymore for fear I'd kill someone because I was crying so hard. I felt as though I was losing my mind. I wanted to escape this horrible city where my daughter had lost her life, and I didn't care where so long as it was far, far away. If I didn't leave soon, I began to fear I'd end up losing my own life.

Very much aware that the Gold Coast had become increasingly unhealthy for me, Stephen began looking around for a new home elsewhere. Our business, Perfect Water Systems, took him to many places stretching from the Gold Coast to Northern New South Wales, a huge stretch scattered with countless small country towns. We had a lot of clients in one of those towns, Warwick, a small community of about fifteen thousand residents about two-and- a-half hours from the Gold

Coast in the Southern Downs, Queensland.

Long story short, Stephen found us a great home there, almost brand-new. We both liked the house, and it ticked all the right boxes, especially its location, so I asked God to give us a sign as to whether we were doing the right thing in buying it. We had inspected the house a couple of time when we noticed something we both took as a sign. From the house's spacious under-roof timber deck, we could see a beautiful church nestled between the trees where it would be visible in all its glory during the day and shine under the moonlight at night, a delightful sight.

We took possession of our new home on the same day the Beijing Olympics started: the 8th of August, 2008 (08/08/08). While the Chinese chose this date because they consider the number eight to be a lucky number, in the Bible this is the designated number that represents resurrection and regeneration, new beginnings, as well as new birth in Christ.

The shape of the number 8, a never-ending loop, is the symbol of eternity. God's law given to Moses in the Old Testament decreed that Jewish boys were to be circumcised on the eighth day. The number eight also represents circumcision of the heart (Romans 2:28-29; Colossians 2:11-13) and becoming a new creation in Christ through the power of the Holy Spirit (2 Corinthians 5:17, Ephesians 2:10; 4:23-24). The numerological values for the letters making up the name Jesus in the Greek add up to 888.

As far as we were concerned, this was no coincidence, but a God-incidence! Also, the previous owners of our new home just happened to be named John and Michelle, the same names as my beloved brother and daughter. We were jumping with joy as we packed up to move, pleased with ourselves for having made the right choice.

Unfortunately, the change did not solve my own struggles. I kept on telling myself that things would improve with time and that the country was good for my grieving phase. But I felt alone and miserable

25 | A 'Country' Change

just as I had back on the Gold Coast.

I must admit this was in part because I failed to reach out to my new community. We'd found a new church with a pastor we really liked. But while we enjoyed the services, I didn't bother to establish new personal relationships. In truth, I could see no valid reason to make an effort anymore. Michelle was gone. She wasn't ever again going to call me to talk or catch up over dinner. Even worse, I would never have the opportunity to say how sorry I was for having said those unkind words and seek her forgiveness.

I was sinking deeper and deeper into the quicksand of depression, and since there was very little anyone could do to stop me, this gradually became a routine in which I felt increasingly comfortable as the days, weeks, and months went by. It was easier to give in to depression than try to fight the impossible, especially since I didn't have the will nor the energy to push my way free from the quicksand.

My problems weren't just mental either. Because I couldn't eat or sleep, the weight was just dropping off me. My immune system was also weakened, so I picked up viruses easily. One day it finally became too much. Making an appointment to see my doctor, I blurted out, "I'm so sick of being sick, Doc! Help me, please!"

With that, I burst into tears. He showed great compassion as I briefly explained what had been going on in my life. He assured me it was quite normal to feel this way after what I had been through. Then he recommended that I see a professional psychologist. Writing me up a referral, he said, "Just give this doctor a go. She's very good in situations like yours."

I procrastinated for several days before finally following my doctor's advice and making an appointment with the psychologist, Mrs. G. It proved to be the best call I had made in months and probably one that saved my life. Once I'd made the appointment, I felt an immediate sense of relief because I knew I couldn't escape my current frame of mind without outside help, and I really needed my sanity to cope with

Adam's upcoming committal hearing.

I went to my appointment with much apprehension as it has always been hard for me to open up to strangers. But to my amazement, Mrs. G was everything the doctor had said she would be. Calm and collected, she let me pour out my pain and grief without judging or interrupting, just nodding here and there when appropriate. A good relationship was formed right from the start, and that meeting was the first of many more to come. She became a big influence on my life, helping me through the various stages of my impossible grief. I don't think I could have ever made a healthy recovery without moving away from the Gold Coast with its memories of Michelle or without Mrs. G's invaluable counselling. Thank you, Mrs. G!

As my mental health improved, I was finally able to drive down to the local shopping center on my own. But I still wasn't out of the woods yet, not by a long shot. Friends and family alike grew more and more concerned as they couldn't see much change in me. Then one day out of the blue, my former sister-in-law, John's ex-wife F*, called to say that she was looking for a travelling companion for an overseas trip. Would I be interested?

Her invitation couldn't have come at a more opportune time. We had a great time together on the trip, and I will always be grateful for that welcome interlude. Still as the trip came to an end, I had to face reality again, especially as Michelle's birthday and the Christmas season approached.

I'd had so many plans for her thirtieth birthday. I even had a special present already tucked away for it. So I struggled to accept we would never enjoy that celebration together. The pain in my heart just didn't seem to ease. I came to realize that, no matter how much time passed, I'd always have trouble getting through the unforgettable dates like anniversaries, birthdays, and Christmases.

With the New Year came some good news regarding the trial. It was scheduled for February 2010 at the Supreme Court in Brisbane.

25 | A 'Country' Change

After more than two years, we'd finally be putting this monster into jail for life and throwing away the key. I just wanted it all to end, but I knew I would need assistance to make it through the ordeal of facing Michelle's murderer. And I got just that. When the day came, I mustered all the strength I could possibly muster and headed to court accompanied by two ladies from the Queensland Homicide Victims Support Group (QHVSG) as well as Jack, Michelle's dad.

Let me stress here that the support offered to me from QHVSG was outstanding. From the very beginning, they assigned a volunteer to call me once a week to make sure I was coping with life without my daughter. I would often sob on the phone for what seemed hours while they patiently listened and tried to understand my pain. I have nothing but respect and admiration for QHVSG because it isn't an easy job, but they do it with a glad heart. These volunteers are truly angels and heroes who deserve a medal for the part they play in helping homicide victims get back on their feet. My deepest thanks, QHVSG!

As I was dressing for court that morning, I received a call from our solicitor stating that the trial might have to be adjourned because the Department of Public Prosecutions (DPP) was seeking further evidence from the T-shirt Michelle had been wearing when she died, which now had to be sent all the way to a forensic lab in Melbourne, Victoria. We headed to court anyway, only to hear from the judge that the trial would indeed be adjourned to a later date.

While the various lawyers and judge were in discussion, I found myself staring at the back of a solidly-built man who was sitting in a glass cubicle, flanked by two policemen. I wasn't sure at first who he might be. Then the penny dropped. Of course, it had to be Adam, although he looked very different from how I remembered him. Prison life obviously agreed with him because he had put on a considerable amount of weight. Nor did he seem at all phased by what was going on around him. He certainly gave no sign of guilt or remorse.

If looks could kill, he would have been dead on the spot. Thank

God he never turned around to look at me. If he had, I would have probably yelled, "Murderer!"

After more than two years, it felt to me that the entire court case had become a charade, especially with this new delay. I wasn't the only one to find it extremely frustrating. As we were leaving the court, the arresting officer, Detective Senior Sergeant P* approached me to express his disappointment over the adjournment.

"Don't worry!" he added consolingly. "He's not going anywhere. I have enough evidence here in these files to put him away for a very, very long time."

Those words alone should have been comforting to me, but they weren't. I had worked at the Sydney Law Courts Library for a couple of years, so I was familiar with how this kind of crime was prosecuted. Jack, a successful criminal defense lawyer, was even more familiar. The problem, as I mentioned earlier, was that the police had still never found the murder weapon, which according to Adam had been Michelle's work belt. So other than Adam's confession, there was no direct proof she'd been strangled vs. death by natural causes or an accident.

And of course, by dumping her body in a wilderness area, he'd also ensured that weather and wild animals would destroy any forensic evidence. In my opinion, that is why he delayed for ten days before finally confessing and leading the police to her makeshift grave. With such a lack of physical evidence, the prosecutors would likely settle for manslaughter. With time already served in jail since the murder, Adam would at most serve five more years in prison.

This all seemed so unjust. At the end of my wits, I cried out to God in despair, pleading, "Please help me because I can't go on like this! You said all I had to do was to forgive him, and you would take care of the rest! 'Let vengeance be mine,' you said to me. Well, I did what you asked. I forgave him. I am taking you at your word. So what now?"

Once again, I heard that now-familiar calm, quiet Voice in my mind, reassuring me, *Trust me, my child!*

25 | A 'Country' Change

I still felt furious, but at the same time calm settled over me in almost a surreal way. I had nothing else to cling on to but God's word, and that was enough.

26

Love and Peace

One Sunday sometime after the trial postponement, our pastor chose the topic of love and the word's many definitions, for that week's sermon. At the end of the morning church service, we were all given a leaflet to take home and meditate on. The leaflet contained a passage from 1 Corinthians 13, often called the "Love Chapter":

> Love is patient, love is kind. It does not envy, it does not boast, it is not proud. It does not dishonor others, it is not self-seeking, it is not easily angered, it keeps no record of wrongs. Love does not delight in evil but rejoices with the truth. It always protects, always trusts, always hopes, always perseveres. Love never fails. (1 Corinthians 13:4-8a)

I reread some of the phrases. *Love does not envy. It is not easily angered. It keeps no record of wrongs. Love does not delight in evil. Love never fails.*

Wow! I found these phrases mind-boggling. The entire passage really described what love is. The question was, could any of us really put these words into practice? Maybe, maybe not.

26 | Love and Peace

Taking out my Bible, I began searching as a cross-reference for other scriptures that spoke of love. I found one in Jesus's Sermon on the Mount that described this same emotion—love—from a different perspective:

> But to you who are listening I say: Love your enemies, do good to those who hate you, bless those who curse you, pray for those who mistreat you ... If you love those who love you, what credit is that to you? Even sinners love those who love them. And if you do good to those who are good to you, what credit is that to you? Even sinners do that ... But love your enemies, do good to them ... Then your reward will be great, and you will be children of the Most High, because he is kind to the ungrateful and wicked. (Luke 6:27-35)

This really showed me personally that love was the key. If I could come to grips with loving even my enemy, someone who had truly mistreated me and shown me hatred in robbing me of my only child, my frame of mind would change altogether.

As I read and reread these verses, I wrestled with the reality that I had to deal with the bad feelings I still harboured towards Adam, or God would not be able to carry out his work in me. I had to let go of the anger I still carried in my heart even after I had chosen to forgive him. Yes, I still wanted justice done. But I had to come to a place where I could truly stop fretting and agonizing over what punishment should be meted out to Adam and just get on with my life.

A new trial date was yet to be scheduled and I was getting restless, not good for the mind at all. A very dear friend of mine, H*, then in her eighties, was very much aware of the pain I had been through and the fiasco regarding the postponed trial. H* had been a colleague when I started work in my early twenties for Sydney's Attorney General department in the Births, Deaths, and Marriages (BD&M) section.

At that time, H* was going through her own time of grief as she had just lost her husband to cancer. She took me under her wing, and over the years we became great friends. She even taught me how to speak "proper-like", since English was still a fairly new language to me back then. She and her husband were childless, but she said to me many times over the years, "You are the daughter we never had."

H* was now planning a trip to Europe, and she felt I needed to get away from it all, so she invited me to accompany her as her companion. As on my prior travels with F*, the trip proved a much-needed time of healing and respite from stress. H* and I had a great time together jaunting through Spain and Portugal and became even stronger, closer friends. I will never forget her kindness.

We returned to Australia early August, only to discover that the trial date was still to be determined. The waiting game continued for the next several months, much to my frustration.

Then one morning in October while I was driving back from a doctor's appointment, my mobile rang. I pulled over to take the call. It was Jack. At first I didn't quite catch what he said. Or maybe I caught it but couldn't quite believe what I'd heard.

"What did you say?" I asked.

"You don't have to worry about the trial anymore," Jack repeated. "Adam has topped himself." [Police speak]

"What do you mean?" I demanded, still not understanding what he was talking about.

"He's dead. He hung himself last night, in his cell."

Wow! I was left totally numb by the news, not knowing whether to laugh or cry because this was not the outcome I had expected. Then I heard again in my mind that calm, quiet Voice reminding me, *Trust Me. I will never leave you, nor forsake you. Let vengeance be mine.*

Well, there it was! In the end, God had taken care of Adam's ultimate punishment, just as he promised. All I had to do was trust in him, no matter what. Lesson learned. We should never question God's ways because they *are* higher than ours!

Composing myself, I completed the drive home, where I told Stephen what had happened. Later that day, Detective Senior Sergeant P* confirmed to us that Adam had committed suicide in his cell the night before, just a month and a bit shy of the third anniversary of Michelle's murder. When the warden found him the next morning, he also found a suicide note Adam had written:

> I'm sorry about all the hurt I caused my family and most importantly what I put Michelle's mother through. I've had enough and I'm getting the f---k out of here.

Though it took three years longer than I'd anticipated, justice had finally been done. My daughter's murderer had received his deserved punishment. But though all now seemed a done deal, it was far from over because I wasn't happy with this outcome.

Okay he's dead now, I kept telling myself. *He'll never hurt another human being again like he did Michelle.*

But I still felt cheated because it seemed Adam had taken the easier, cowardly way out. He should be spending the rest of his life in jail for taking an innocent life. That he was dead with no more suffering for his crime seemed unfair. Yes, I had forgiven him. Yes, I'd asked God to help me love my enemy. But shouldn't he still have to pay for what he'd done?

Then I began to recognize just how much guilt must have been invading Adam's mind in all the months he sat in prison. Guilt reflected in his suicide note, not only for what he'd done to Michelle, but the agony through which he'd put me as her mother as well as the shame and pain his own family was suffering.

I suddenly realized this was exactly what I'd asked God to do when I found out that Adam had strangled my Michelle. I'd prayed that her murderer would see my daughter's face from the moment he woke up in the morning until he went to sleep at night as a reminder of his cowardly, brutal act. And God had answered my prayer. He'd also kept his word to me that he would handle Adam's punishment.

In the end, that constant reminder of his crime against such a beautiful human being could have led Adam to repentance and redemption. Instead, like Judas, the betrayer of Jesus, he'd allowed the guilt to build up until it had driven him mad, leading him to take his own life. But that had been his choice, not any vengeance of mine. He had paid for her life with his own. Even worse, he would be paying the price for all eternity for his unrepentant sin. You couldn't have asked for greater justice.

As for me, I could testify honestly that I didn't hate Adam, though I despised his brutal action that ended my daughter's life. I had forgiven him a long time ago, just as God had asked of me. And I came to realize he must have been a pretty messed up individual to let himself be consumed by jealousy to the point of murdering the woman he loved.

So case closed, but not by any means over. This long-drawn-out drama inevitably took a toll on my health. As the years passed, certain dates would trigger anxiety attacks and uncontrollable sobbing that left me with renewed trauma. My doctors cautioned me repeatedly to avoid stress at all costs.

Easier said than done!

27

New Storms Ahead

Following Adam's suicide, Detective Senior Sergeant P* contacted Stephen to arrange for him to pick up those things of Michelle's that had been held by the police to use as evidence at the trial. Since the trial never resumed, the detective thought I might like to have them back. As Stephen chatted with the detective, they talked about the vision God had given us regarding the location of Michelle's remains.

"Do you remember that?" Stephen asked.

"Stephen, I will never forget it!" the detective replied. He was not a church-goer, but the event had definitely changed his attitude towards God and the reality of God's working and miracles. We prayed that any seeds of faith planted through this experience would bear fruit.

Christmas was once again a blur as it had been so for the last three years, but I was gradually settling into a new "normal", if I could call it that. But now it was my mother's health that was changing. She was becoming weaker day by day, and the realization that the inevitable could be near frightened me.

Another year slipped through my fingers, and Mum was getting ready to go on her annual overseas holiday. I flew down to Sydney to help her pack as well as spend some quality time with her. Jack, my ex, had always been very fond of Mum and popped in as he often did to wish her a good holiday. Sadly, during her holiday, Jack was diagnosed with an aggressive brain cancer and died less than two months later. My poor Mum was shocked by the news and took it very hard.

That next year in March 2013, Mum turned ninety-three years old. Though a couple of bad falls had lessened her mobility, she was determined to take her annual overseas holiday. She was travelling with my brother Tony, who had been her companion and care-giver since my father's passing, as well as my sister Gloria. I flew to Sydney to see her off, as was my ritual. Knowing how frail and unwell she was, I had the feeling this might possibly be her last trip, so I cherished every moment with her.

Sure enough, the long flight to France took a toll on Mum, and, as soon as they arrived at my sister Lily's place, she was taken straight to hospital. Once she was well enough to travel, Mum, Tony, and Lily continued on to Portugal by car, where they spent the next three months at our family homestead.

Glad as Mum was to be back where all her children were born, her health continued to deteriorate, necessitating frequent hospital visits. But she was determined to travel back to France with Tony, Lily, and Gloria to return the car rental and say a last goodbye to family members there before flying back to Australia. Sadly, by the time they arrived in October 2013, she once again had to be taken to the hospital.

It was evident to all Mum was ready to embark on her final journey to heaven, where she would be pain-free with her Saviour. But she also wanted to hang on just a little longer as her youngest child—me—wasn't there to say goodbye. In fact, I was the only one of her children back in Australia at that crucial time.

I immediately set about booking the next flight available. But just as happened with my brother John, I received a call from Tony telling me it was too late. Mum was gone. I should have been expecting it, but I wasn't because I just couldn't imagine my world without my Mum.

27 | New Storms Ahead

"Why God? Why did you take my Mum, my rock, my strength?" I screamed heavenward. "How can I go on without her? Who is going to listen to my problems and always make me feel better? How can I go on? God, help me. Please, HELP ME!"

Being her only child not there to say goodbye really hit me hard, and I ended up in the hospital with an acute anxiety attack that had the same symptoms of a heart attack. The doctors were adamant that I shouldn't travel overseas, let alone to my mother's funeral, as the shock and devastation would be too much for me to bear.

But I was determined that if her youngest child couldn't be there when Mum left this planet, nothing was going to keep me from her funeral. This would be held in Portugal as her wish was to be laid to rest in the family crypt with Dad and John. My brother John's son A* and Gloria's daughter A* were also travelling from Sydney to say farewell to their grandmother, and that was all the encouragement I needed, since they could keep an eye on me in case of another anxiety attack.

So with Stephen's blessing, my two bodyguards, and the right medication to manage the stress, I made it to Portugal to say a last farewell to my Mum. But her loss put me right back into the dark pit I had been in before. Even though I still had my three "boys" (Stephen, Sunny Boy, and Prince), I felt alone. With Mum gone, my trips to Sydney became less frequent, and I must admit I missed them. Depression lurked like a bad smell, which meant that the anxiety attacks were not far away, needing only a trigger to bring on the uncontrollable sobs.

"Don't fret Mum!" I could hear Michelle telling me. "Calm down!"

But how could I not fret? I just couldn't help myself. I felt totally powerless, unable to control my emotions. Something was wrong, but I didn't know what.

In contrast, my doctor waved it off as normal given the circumstances, insisting, "It will get better in time."

I wasn't so sure. And indeed, unbeknownst to me, I was about to embark on one more major roller-coaster in a life already overflowing with them. In March 2014, Stephen made an appointment with his doctor for a general check-up, and I opted to come along. At the end of the consultation, I asked the doctor if he would look at something that was troubling me at the back of my tongue. It had been there for a couple of years, but my prior doctors had dismissed it, saying it was just part of my tonsils.

But this doctor took me seriously. It could be a cyst, he told me, and it would be prudent to have it checked out. So we made an appointment with the specialist he recommended, who agreed it was a cyst.

"We have two options," the specialist told me. "We can remove it and do a biopsy, or just watch to see if it grows. Which would you prefer."

"Please remove it," I responded. "I've had this thing for a couple of years already, and I would like it out as soon as possible!"

The operation was scheduled four weeks later. I'd been told to expect some serious pain for a few days after the procedure, and indeed it did hurt and my tongue itself turned black-and-blue. But as far as I was concerned, the whole exercise had been worth it because the cyst was now out of my body.

We still had to wait for the biopsy results. This took almost a week, and when the results came back, it wasn't good news. The pathologist had concluded it was a carcinoma, i.e., a cancer that begins in the outer epithelial tissue of the skin, in my case the tongue. Devastated, I burst into tears right there in the doctor's office.

Surgery was scheduled for the following month, May 2014. When I came out of the anesthesia, I found myself in agony. The sides of my mouth were split open and blistered while numerous tubes were connected to my mouth and body. I couldn't recall ever having experienced such pain in my life, and I prayed to God that I never would again. For days, I could neither eat nor speak.

27 | New Storms Ahead

The good news was that the doctors had been able to get all the cancer, praise God! But in the midst of all this, I wanted to talk to my mum. Six months ago, she would have been on phone, reassuring me, "It's going to be okay, darling. God is going to fix it. I'll pray up a storm for you. Don't worry, child. I won't let anything happen to you."

As with Michelle, I had to face the reality that I would not hear those words again because my mum was gone. My siblings Tony and Gloria, were supportive, but they were far away in Sydney, so they couldn't visit me in the hospital. Thank God Stephen was there for me the entire week I was there, or I would most definitely not have been able to cope. Stephen also got busy asking all his email buddies for prayer as well as our local church. I was blessed with countless "get well" wishes and flowers to boot.

The hospital released me on Mother's Day, a sweet reminder that Mum and Michelle would be thinking of me from heaven and maybe even looking down on me, since Scripture references the "great cloud of witnesses", those who have gone before us, watching our own spiritual race from heaven (Hebrews 12:1-2). That in itself on such a very significant day gave me the strength I needed to get better.

My recovery was slow, but my tongue soon started to regenerate. What an amazing organ. My surgeon explained to me that because the tongue is always wet, this promotes regeneration. Even though it would never grow back to exactly what it had been, this was music to my ears. While I have been subject ever since to quarterly check-ups, so far so good!

A word of advice, if I may. Embrace life with open arms because every day is a bonus. I give all glory for my restored health to God. He is omnipotent, omniscient, and omnipresent (all-powerful, all-knowing, and present everywhere). I had faith from the beginning that it was God's will to heal me from this cancer, and that is what he did, thank you Jesus!

28

Duty of Care

On my first day back home from my operation, I was resting in bed when I heard the phone ring. Since I couldn't speak, Stephen took the call on my behalf. It was Detective Senior Sergeant P* on the phone. I was curious as it was now going on seven years since Michelle's death and a long time since we had heard from the detective.

It turned out that he was calling to let us know that the Brisbane Times were going to publish an article on the seven worst murders that had shocked Queensland over the past ten years. Michelle's was on top of the list. Detective Senior Sergeant P* had called as a courtesy to advise us of what was about to unfold. He hadn't been aware of my operation and made sure to convey through Stephen his apologies over the article and best wishes for my speedy recovery.

To me, the article felt like rubbing salt into my wounds since publishing it certainly wouldn't improve anything as far as I was concerned, and I would rather not have known about it at all. I continued my daily routine, which was mainly just lying in bed and convalescing while trying to deal with the excruciating pain I was enduring. Since I couldn't speak clearly at this point, I would often express my feelings to God silently, knowing he could hear me just as well as though I were voicing them audibly.

God, how long is this going to last? I would demand. *I can't stand it anymore! You know the pain killers aren't working, so would you help me please!*

There would be only silence. So I would repeat, *Didn't you hear me, Lord?*

Then one day instead of silence, I heard that now-familiar Voice respond as clearly as though speaking aloud, "I will heal you, and when it happens, I want you to tell your story."

What do you mean, my story? I asked, sure I wasn't hearing right. *I'm not a gifted speaker! What am I to say?*

"Don't worry. I will give you the words. Just do it!"

For a moment, I had no doubt I had just heard God's voice speaking audibly to me. Then I shook it off and told myself, *Don't be silly, woman! You were dreaming!*

But a few days later, I heard the Voice again. "Just do it!"

Caught unaware, I immediately blurted out, *Okay! If you say so!*

At this point, I decided it was time to share with Stephen what I had been hearing over the last couple of days. He had no doubt it was God's Holy Spirit speaking to me.

"Wow! If that's the case, then it's simple," he told me. "You must be obedient."

"Hang on a minute!" I responded, having difficulty articulating my words since my mouth was still in great pain. "God never spoke to me like that before. He's given me visions in my sleep such as the one about Michelle's location. But I have never heard his voice out loud before! Surely, I must have been dreaming, right?"

Time went by, and I was gradually getting back to my old self. The pain eventually subsided, and as my tongue and mouth healed, I was once again able to articulate well, much to my relief. In all this, I couldn't forget the words I had heard. Perhaps God wanted me to share my story at church. Yes, that must be it! I was sure of it. What else could it have been?

So when I was feeling better and able to attend church again,

Stephen had a word with our pastor, who readily agreed to give me a few minutes to share my story with his congregation. Okay, this sounded like a good plan and one easy enough to execute.

But what happened when I got up to speak was very different than I had anticipated. The moment I was given the microphone, I froze and couldn't utter a single word. Then I began wobbling like a fragile branch in the wind. Thank God the pastor caught me as I fell. When I recovered consciousness, I muttered to myself, "Well done! How embarrassing was that? You really made a fool of yourself, didn't you?"

Clearly this was not what God had in mind when he spoke to me. I had to concede that public speaking was not for me, and that was that. I never broached the subject again with the pastor nor pursued the matter further in any other context. I turned my focus instead on continuing to get better in God's time so I could go back to the new normal that had been my life since Michelle's demise. And though I was still grieving the loss of my mum as well, I knew that with God's help and in the power of the Holy Spirit I could do this.

Puppy was also helping me every step of the way. As always, he was so loving towards me. I was so preoccupied with my own recovery that I neglected at first to notice that my precious doggy's health was declining rapidly. First, our daily walks became something of a chore for him, which alone should have triggered alarm bells in my head. He was also becoming deafer by the day and could no longer see past his nose. He had other medical issues, not just the normal signs of old age, but a lot of discomfort and pain as well.

It was pitiful to see him like this. Stephen and I had always been committed never to let our pets suffer, and I couldn't help but remember how we had struggled when making a similar decision regarding our other two beloved collies, Shadow and Mr. Biscuits. They were wonderful dogs, but in Prince we'd had the best of the other two combined. There are no words that do him justice. He was a gift from God when we most needed him, plain and simple.

28 | Duty of Care

But now we knew the time had come for our darling little "Prince of Peace" to meet his Maker. Over the next days, we went out of our way to make him as comfortable and happy as we possibly could, buying him the best doggie treats, taking extra care with his grooming, and in general treating him like the prince he was.

On the appointed day, Stephen drove us to the vet while I sat in the back seat with Prince. He put his head lovingly on my lap as though he was at complete peace without a worry in the world. As the vet did his part, Stephen and I kept stroking Prince and telling him how much we loved him. Tears streamed down my face onto Prince as his breathing finally stopped. His eyes were still fixed lovingly on me, and from a corner of one eye, a tear spilled down. Whether his or one of mine, it looked as though he'd shed a tear for us.

Stephen had the same reaction. "Look, Prince is crying for us!"

I will never forget that scene. It was as though Puppy was letting us know that he felt our pain, telling us, "I know you love me, Mummy and Daddy, and I love you too. And I understand you have to do this. Don't worry about me; it's all good. You were my God-appointment for these past years, and now my job is done. It's time to let me go."

The following weeks and months were unbearable to say the least. My sorrow was inconsolable as was Stephen's. This was precisely the type of stress the doctors had warned me to avoid lest it trigger another acute anxiety attack. Sure enough, one day I suddenly experienced a severe pain in my left arm. The main veins were so swollen I thought they were going to explode.

"Oh, no, I'm having a heart attack!" I yelled.

Stephen immediately drove me to the emergency room of our local hospital, where I underwent a series of tests including an ultrasound of the veins in my left arm to make sure there were no lingering blood clots. I was eventually released with a caution to avoid stress.

This wasn't so easy with my beautiful Prince gone. I knew some people out there might be saying, "He was just a dog!" But he wasn't to us. He was the most loyal, loving companion anyone could ever ask for, and it was a privilege to have been part of his life. Any of you, my readers, who have had a close canine companion know exactly what I mean.

It has now been three years since Prince left us. And though we still miss him, we also know God sent him to us for a very specific reason and season to help us with our grief, mine to be more specific. As one friend later expressed, "You may have rescued him, but in all reality he rescued you!"

But that sad loss wasn't the end. As with Mr. Biscuits, I was sure no other animal could ever replace Prince, and of course each of our canine "children", still holds a special place in our hearts, as you, dear reader, will understand if you have loved and lost a pet. But Stephen and I still have plenty of love to make another animal feel wanted, and about a year ago—two years after losing Prince—we decided it was time for another four-legged friend. Again, we chose a rescue dog as we wanted to help an animal in need find his "fur'ever" home. But as collies are high maintenance, we opted this time for something small, white, and fluffy that would fit into an oversized handbag.

God led us to an adorable Shih Tzu mix we named Xavier. He is Mr. Personality, and life never holds a dull moment around him. Once again we're a complete little family, and I can't stop smiling. In fact, not long after we picked up our precious little bundle of fun, a neighbour mentioned to Stephen, "I haven't seen your wife this happy in a long time. She looks ten years younger."

That's got to be a good thing in itself, right? Who doesn't want to look younger! One of the proverbs written thousands of years ago by the wise King Solomon reminds:

A cheerful heart is good medicine, but a crushed spirit dries up the bones. (Proverbs 17:22)

I can testify that trading my crushed, despairing spirit for a heart filled with love and joy has given me a new lease on life. I am now embracing the future with both arms and have absolute faith and confidence that happy days are ahead, hallelujah!

EPILOGUE

Well, dear reader, this is where I finish sharing my story. Not that it has come to an end. My story will go on into eternity, just as yours will. But if I don't stop writing now, this book could go on forever. You never know, there could just be a sequel in the making!

In these pages, I have shared the most intimate details of my life story with all of its pain, grief, and loss as well as my own failings because I truly believe that is what God has called me to do. What I haven't yet shared is that God's call on my heart to tell my story began long before Michelle's tragic death and just a few years after I gave my heart to Jesus Christ.

By this time, Stephen and I were living in Queensland and had started our own business working from home. Every morning, I would go for a brisk walk around the neighbourhood where we lived. As I walked, I would chat with my heavenly Father, praying over our needs, family situation, or just talking to God.

One day as I was walking, completely out of the blue, God revealed to me a vivid image, much as he revealed to Stephen and me all those years later where Michelle's body could be found. I was stunned by the vision, especially since I was wide awake, not in bed dreaming. In the image, I was being ushered into a big hall full of people. Stephen was waiting there for me, and someone was introducing me to the crowd.

Epilogue

That was where the vision ended. But a couple of days later, I had the same vision. I couldn't understand the meaning of it, especially since I am extremely shy when it comes to public speaking, as you already know. But I also knew this was real, not a dream or hallucination. Nothing further came of that image, so I eventually put it out of my mind and thought no more of it for several years.

Then came my convalescence from my carcinoma operation, long after Michelle's death, when God made clear that he wanted me to tell my story, as I shared with you in an earlier chapter. Only then did I connect that earlier vision with the heavenly "chats" I was having with God during my recovery from cancer. At the time, I believed the vision meant I was to share my story from a church platform. You know how that turned out!

In time, I came to realize that God was calling me to *write* my story, not just speak to an audience. And I had to be obedient to that call, not for my glory but his. You are now reading the result of my obedience. Maybe as God leads, that original vision of being introduced in front of a crowd of people will still happen on some future date after this book is published. I have seen so many others of God's revelations come true.

Meanwhile, it is my hope and prayer that in these pages you have caught a glimpse of how greatly and lovingly God has helped me through the highs and lows of my life, especially in the loss of my beautiful Michelle. And God can be your friend and confidant as well, my dear reader, but only if you let him. Our Creator is a gentleman. He doesn't force his way into our lives and hearts, but waits to be invited, as he tells us in the very last book of the Bible, Revelations:

> Here I am! I stand at the door and knock. If anyone hears my voice and opens the door, I will come in and eat with that person, and they with me. (Revelations 3:20).

But once you do open your heart door to let him in, your heavenly Father, your Lord and Saviour, will never leave you. That's his promise to us all (Joshua 1:9, Isaiah 41:10-13, Matthew 28:20, Hebrews 13:5). As you get to know him intimately as I have, you'll be able to feel his loving, comforting arms around you when it matters the most and when nothing else will do.

I started this book telling you about my hidden thorns. I may have been graced at birth with the name Rose with all the sweet fragrance, beautiful colours, and silky softness that it may evoke. But over the decades, I've learned only too well how deceptive appearances can be and how sharp and painful are the thorns a rose hides under its outward beauty. My hidden thorns are not just the outward tragedies I've endured, but as I've shared honestly from the beginning, thorns of my own doing—whether personal shortcomings, failure, or sin.

Like the apostle Paul when he begged God to take away his own hidden thorn (2 Corinthians 12:7-10), mine are still there. I am still far from a perfect person, and my sorrow over the unjust, cruel way my Michelle was stolen from me will never completely dissipate. In fact, sometimes it feels as though accepting her death becomes even more difficult as I get older.

I'm sure you, my reader, can identify, as let's not kid ourselves, we all have hidden thorns. It's the way we deal with them that makes all the difference. And just as God's grace was sufficient for the apostle Paul in his weakness (v. 9), so God's Holy Spirit gives me strength and comfort when times get hard. While my thorns are still there, thanks to God's working in my life, I can testify they are much more pruned back and sanded down now, so they don't hurt as much. God will do the same for you if you let him.

The tenth anniversary of my baby girl's murder is now behind me. How do I feel? Time does heal up to a certain point, and I can say truthfully that there is peace in my heart for I have chosen to look at this year as a new blessing full of promises for a brighter future. A wise

Epilogue

person once said, "The past is but a reference library; it's not a place to live in."

That is so true. As I see it, a key to sanity and being able to move on is accepting that we may never know this side of eternity why certain things happen in our lives. Why God allows them to happen. But we can still embrace each new day God gives us, leaving the past where it belongs—in the past.

Please allow me to share with you one final anecdote that illustrates how God has impacted my life thus far. Recently I had reason to visit an oral specialist, Professor J*. The last time I had been in his dental practice was almost eleven years prior in September 2007, which was several months after my brother John's passing but before my daughter Michelle's murder.

As we dealt with the reason for my appointment, Professor J* expressed interest as to what had been going on in my life since we last met. Guessing that he was unaware of the murder, I explained what had happened as well as my carcinoma operation, family deaths, and other tragic events of recent years. He stared at me with horror, then exclaimed with shocked dismay, "No, that's terrible!"

After a short pause, he went on, "Well, looking at you now, no one would ever know all you've been through. If I may say so, you look remarkably well and joyful. Tell me, what are you taking for it? Which antidepressants are you on?"

I shook my head. "I'm not on anything, Professor. My faith in our Lord Jesus Christ is what has carried me through one day at a time. I would have gone insane without that."

Please let me make clear here that my own choice is not meant to be in any way critical of anyone who has been medically prescribed antidepressants. Just as God answered my prayer for healing from carcinoma, even though for his own reasons and in his sovereignty he did not choose to heal my brother John or prevent Michelle's brutal murder, so God in his grace has given me emotional and spiritual healing without any dependence on medications, and for that I am so thankful.

As we were talking, the professor in turn confided that his own wife had recently passed away, a grief he was still dealing with. I happened to mention in passing that I was writing a book about Michelle's murder and how my faith in God helped me through my darkest days. I also shared my reasons for writing. Above all, my hope of helping others who have experienced similar loss and trauma so they too can tap into the very same Source that is my lifeline, our Creator God and heavenly Father, and in so doing receive relief and comfort in him.

"That's wonderful. You are quite a woman, Marie-Rose, remarkable even!" the professor told me. "When the book is finished, please send me a copy. I'll be very interested in reading it."

At that moment I felt only the beauty and sweet fragrance of my namesake, no longer its prickly thorns. I pray that the professor and countless others may indeed benefit from reading my story. Including you, my dear reader.

My heartfelt thanks to you for picking up this book and joining me on my journey. It isn't over yet. As I write this last page, I have let go of the past with its anger, grief, bitterness, and pain and am looking forward to each new day with hope, joy, and expectations. It is now time to smell the roses and not worry about their thorns. It is time to embrace the future with both hands for as many days and years ahead as God grants me here in this beautiful country of Australia with my loving husband, family, church community, and friends.

And in God's time and choosing, one of those days will be my last this side of eternity. Then I will step through heaven's gates to be welcomed by my beautiful Christmas angel—my precious daughter Michelle—along with my brother John, Mum and Dad, and so many other brothers and sisters in God's kingdom. And of course, my Creator, my loving heavenly Father, my Lord and Saviour Jesus Christ.

Epilogue

Then my journey will be complete.
Then I will be truly healed.
Then I will be home.

ABOUT THE AUTHOR

Marie-Rose Fox was born in Portugal. She relocated with her family to France, where she spent most of her teenage years. Whilst there, she developed a great love for languages as a challenge (Portuguese, French, Spanish, Italian and English). At just eighteen she immigrated with her family to Australia, where they lived in the Eastern Suburbs of Sydney. She resided within this community for most of her adult life until she met and married Stephen. Circumstances led them to live on the Gold Coast of Queensland, where they met with tragedy in 2007 when her only child, Michelle was brutally murdered.

As a consequence of this horrific ordeal, she suffered deep depression, so given the need for change she and her husband chose a country lifestyle for a season. As a reader of this 'all telling book of her life' you'll be glad to hear she climbed out of her 'black hole' of depression through her faith and love for God.

www.ingramcontent.com/pod-product-compliance
Lightning Source LLC
Chambersburg PA
CBHW031419290426
44110CB00011B/454